The Station

A Journey of Discovery

By

Ileana Ramos

Second Edition

Library of Congress Control Number: 2005932391

First Edition ©2006 by Ileana Ramos

Second Edition ©2020 by Ileana Ramos

ISBN-13: 978-1-7345070-0-3

Second Edition Note: This book has been revised to reflect changes of perception in the writer's thinking since 2005 when the original book was written. Even though the core of the story has not changed, the language and presentation has been somewhat modified.

For more information or to order additional books,
please visit my website at: www.Ileanawrites.com

Dedication

This book is dedicated to you, dear reader.
I believe in my heart that it's no coincidence that you
have been led to read it.

Special Dedication

This book is dedicated with great love, respect, admiration, and thanksgiving
to the memory of my beloved mentor and friend, Albert Kearns, who through
his own example showed me the way.

Special Acknowledgment

Life provided me with the absolute perfect editor to assist me with the second revision of this manuscript. It is with great humbleness and heartfelt thanks that I appreciate the outstanding job Frank Butler did on the editing of this revision. I am so grateful for all his hard work and for the great suggestions he contributed.

I also wish to thank Joanna Butler for her wonderful recommendations and contributions to this edition.

Acknowledgment

I wish to thank Carol Showalter for her encouragement and moral support during the writing of the original book. I appreciate her patiently reading and listening to the drafts. Her assistance in the development of this manuscript was invaluable, and it has made my dream come true.

I also wish to acknowledge Michelle Bauer for her unconditional willingness in helping me with the creation of the original book. Her assistance was greatly appreciated, and her friendship is a treasure of the heart.

I wish to thank Susan Buck for the outstanding work she did editing the first edition.

The book to read is not the one which thinks for you,
but the one which makes you think.

James McCosh

Table of Contents

Prologue

Life is a mystery that demands to be explored.

Dostoyevsky

Most of the sold-out crowd were at the theater before the doors opened. They had heard about the story called The Station, and tonight was the night!

Tony was in the dressing room, awaiting the signal. He had earned a reputation for being one of the best storytellers in town; but tonight he was a little nervous. He would have to be at his very best, because this story was *different*. This presentation required a special kind of narrator - someone who truly knew the subject. He would have to explain the truths hidden in the story, and also share directly from his own life experiences. Deep down, he was confident that he was the right person to deliver the message.

He heard the stage manager shout through the door, "Five minutes!"

The audience was eager and attentive. The Announcer appeared, welcomed them, and told them they were in for an evening of inspiration. At last, the curtains opened. Tony smiled as he walked out into the spotlight to loud applause. He sat down in the leather chair and took off his hat. He was ready.

Chapter One: The Decision

Tony

It is a pleasure to be here this evening, said Tony, brimming with confidence and self-assurance.

Tony paused and gazed at the audience.

I don't know what it is you are searching for in your life. Many of us search for peace of mind and peace of heart. We want rest for our souls. To find these things—peace of mind and peace of heart—in the midst of this alarming world in which we live, is a gift that cannot be compared to any earthly pleasures. To have tranquility, harmony, and serenity in your heart is a priceless treasure.

We need and want peace of mind. Peace of mind—what a jewel! Can this jewel actually be found in a world of so many quarrels and so much hopelessness, chaos and danger?

Multitudes are seeking peace in recognition and wealth, in happiness and power, in education and knowledge, in human relationships and romantic love. People desire to fill their heads with knowledge and their pockets with money, but their hearts remain unfulfilled and their souls empty.

The Station invites you to take a journey through its pages, through the soul and mind of Lily, an ordinary person, who was starving for the light of the Spirit. At times you may identify with Lily, and at other times, you may not. Either way, I hope you enjoy this story. Although it involves fiction, it also contains great truths that cannot be denied. If you listen to this story—without prejudice or criticism—you may find hidden jewels that can enrich your life.

Now, relax and allow me to take you to *The Station*, where we'll ride on the trains that will take us through the hills and valleys of this story. It will be my great honor to hold your hand and take you on this journey.

Shall we begin?

What would be something worse than to be blind?
To be blind in the spirit!

Helen Keller

Tony	What a beautiful day it is. Beautiful indeed—even though the sky is blue in some areas and gray in others.

> Tony looked out at the audience. The same goes for our lives. Sometimes things are good; sometimes they are not. As a result of my own spiritual journey, I have been able to discern that in order to grow as an individual, I've needed to learn that the ups and downs of my life are lessons that will allow me to reach that place of freedom that I've yearned so much to find.

The mountains seem calm and quiet, standing still, displaying their majesty.

> Tony paused. This is the way I long to be... calm and quiet, displaying the peace of the Spirit.

The sound of a river can be heard coming forth from its source, running like a torrent toward the ocean in search of its final destination.

> Tony closed his eyes for a brief moment. This river reminds me of my own soul, desperate to be in union with the source of my creation.

The birds are flying free under the open sky, allowing nature to provide for their needs.

> Tony stopped.

> This is what I long for—to be free of the pressures of the world and to believe wholeheartedly that all of my needs will be met. As I go along on the path of my life, I am beginning to comprehend that I cannot be free until I find in my own heart, the truth of my existence.

The trees are tall, tranquil, unaltered by their surroundings even though their leaves are changing colors.

> Our lives also change colors. More often than not, we are overwhelmed by the change. It is not so with the trees. They remain still, firm, strong, and beautiful through the change. Surely it's because they are in total union with the earth, knowing what they are and to whom they belong.

The garden is full of gorgeous flowers, so beautiful and perfect. How could the existence of God even be denied? They are all different and unique, created in special forms and dressed in splendid colors.

When I stop to admire the flowers, I think of the human race. We are so different from one another, yet each one has a particular kind of beauty that needs to be discovered. The fact that we cannot see beauty in everyone does not mean that it isn't there.

Tony sighed... What a magnificent place this is!

Let your eyes gently close. Allow the eyes of your imagination to open. Can you see it?

Think today, and speak tomorrow.

H.C. Bohn

Tony	There she was, standing in front of the vast ocean. At the time, Lily was only eight years old. She was gazing at the waves spilling onto the shore, feeling the sun on her face and tasting the salty breeze.
Lily thought	Where does all this come from?
Tony	As her life moved forward and she grew up, other questions came into her heart.
Lily thought	Who am I? What am I doing here? What am I supposed to do with my life? I need answers.
Tony	Lily began to experience an intense inner hunger to find answers to these questions, and so her journey for the truth began. It wasn't going to be an easy road because a spiritual path has many twists and turns. First, Lily will need to wake up to her spirituality so she can become acquainted with heights to which she can ascend.

She will have to come face to face with the fact that she is mistaken—just like I used to be—living her life with unreasonable ideas about the meaning of love, happiness, joy, and everything else. Many of them are ideas imposed on us by society. Lily will have to understand that no one can define the truth for her, because the truth can only be found in her heart. In order to find the truth, Lily will need to be open and willing to listen. I have learned that to be open does not mean being naïve. It does not simply mean accepting at face value whatever someone else is saying. To be open means to be willing to change. It means accepting that perhaps our own belief system is wrong, that we have accepted ideas that have been influencing our lives and steering us in the wrong path.

Out of suffering have emerged the strongest souls.

Edwin Hubbel Chapin

Tony	The alarm went off. Lily opened her eyes to a brand new day.
Lily thought	Oh no, not another day...
Tony	All she wanted was to stay in her bed. She had no desire to get up. The weight of the world was upon her shoulders. Lily was depressed. She felt rejected and betrayed. The pain of her soul was so intense that on many occasions it was more than she could take. It hurt. *It hurt a lot!* Lily did not want to go on living. She was sad, angry and confused.
Lily thought	Is this what life is all about?
Tony	All she wanted was love, and love eluded her over and over again. The alarm went off once more.
	Time to get up and wear the mask. It was a thick one—so thick that nobody could ever suspect she was hurting. She was putting on a great act. Lily did not allow anyone to see her pain. It was too embarrassing to be weak and to admit that love had abandoned her.
Lily thought	I don't need you!
Tony	Lily's heart was broken. A grey blanket of grief was wrapped around her soul. Lily had loved and trusted, just like a child does, and one day her heart was crushed into millions of pieces, just like a building crumbles when it has no foundation. The truth is that Lily was a very fortunate person. She had so much going for her, but she was blind. She could not discern the great gifts she had in her life. She was lost in the darkness of her soul, dragging from one place to the next the emptiness of her heart. All she wanted was to love and to be loved. Yet love had no plans to stick around. Lily felt sad and alone. Loneliness was her companion—a companionship that hurt her soul so intensely. Needless to say, Lily was angry—very angry in fact. She was furious at the world. Over and over, she told herself:

Lily thought	I don't need anybody. I can do everything alone...
Tony	She was building a thick wall around her to shield herself from her nasty world.

Lily was engulfed with rage and bitterness, apprehension and confusion, frustration and despair. She was frightened of not knowing what the future held and not being certain where to go next. She wished to be free from the despair she felt in her soul, but she had no clue as to how to find freedom. Lily had no place to go. She did not wish to let others know about her pain. That was all she had—other people—who not only were as blind as she was, but also were too busy to take the time to listen to her lonely soul. For the most part, people didn't understand. All they wanted to do was talk, judge, and give advice. They were not able to listen. She felt so alone and helpless. She had tried many times to find the answers in her own mind and even discern them from the thoughts of others. She tried to use her own power to heal herself from the emptiness of her heart, all with little avail.

Lily wanted to be in control of her circumstances. She wanted to be the master of her life, the captain of her ship. She wanted things the way she wanted them and when she wanted them. This was the origin of her pain. She longed for peace and joy, but she was a perfectionist. This made things worse for her since the need for perfection and the desire for inner peace clash with each other. Lily wasn't aware that those desiring these things in their lives must learn and understand, deep in their hearts, that in the big picture, what they want doesn't really matter.

This makes me think of my friend and mentor, Keith. I had been a perfectionist myself and insisted that things should be exactly how I wanted them to be, instead of how they were. During one of our heart-to-heart discussions, he said to me:

Keith	Tony, the day you stop living your life based on 'I want this' or 'I don't want that' or 'I like that' or 'I don't like this,' you will find it. When you master your need for perfection, you will understand that life is just right as it is. When you constantly worry about things you cannot change, you are losing touch with the magic and beauty that life has to offer.
Tony	In her heart, Lily knew that there was something else—a special place where she belonged. She was searching for such a place. She was searching for the fountain, the source of

love, peace, joy, rest, understanding, and the answers to the mystery of her life.

What a rebellious spirit she carried! She did not appreciate being told what to do, how to live her life, to have someone interpret for her the mystery of man's existence. She desired to find the answers alone—in her own heart. She longed to have the freedom to choose her own truth in the way that she better understood it. She was tired of being manipulated like a marionette, with events or people telling her how to feel. She wanted to be free... free to be. Lily was determined to find the way on her own, to walk her own path, and to learn her own lessons. That was her right. She owed it to herself to explore her life and find the food to nourish her broken spirit.

Demand not that events should happen as you wish,
but wish them to happen as they do,
and you will go on well.

-Epictetus

Tony	It was storming outside. The rain was pouring down. Lily was looking at the raindrops making shiny trails as they ran down her window glass.
Lily thought	Just like the storm that's raging in my soul and the tears falling from my heart...
Tony	She was tired, tired of living so empty, tired of failed relationships, tired of feeling angry and insecure, tired of not knowing what to do, of walking towards places that didn't nourish her thirsty soul. She was weary of pretending she was happy, of projecting an image that was so far from the truth. She wished she could remove the mask that she always wore to hide her true identity. Lily suffered due to the powerlessness she felt because things didn't work out her way. She wanted to free herself from the manipulation she exercised on other people in order to fulfill her own needs. She felt unprepared to face the adversities of her life, and had no firm foundation to build on.

Closing her eyes in despair, she cried. She was desperate to be in union with the source of her creation and be held in its invisible arms. She was longing for the fountain. She needed to find meaning and purpose in her life. |
| Lily thought | Where is the fountain? |

Tony

She needed to find the arms where she could rest from the demands of the world, from the pressure she placed on her own self, from her own thoughts and beliefs that kept her in bondage.

Lily knew there was a long journey ahead of her She realized that all her efforts to heal the emptiness of her soul had been futile. And now, she had the desire—the burning need—to move forward, to reach out and search for wisdom and knowledge. She decided to take a journey through the landscape of her soul and her mind, hoping to find the cure. She wanted to be rid of the obstacles she had placed there herself, that blocked the flow of the living waters.

As Lily moves from one place to the next in her journey, she will discover eminent truths that are imperative in order to find the spirit of peace. She will be faced with truths about herself that she will not particularly like. But nevertheless, if her priority is to find peace of mind and peace of heart, she will have no choice but to accept the challenges that she will encounter along the way and then take action.

Chapter Two: Knowledge City

Forgiveness is man's deepest need and highest achievement.

Horace Bushnell

Tony

With her heart bursting with pain, from fear, insecurity, rejection, frustration, lack of willpower, resentment, and anger, Lily reached the station. The train was to take her to the fountain. Feeling absolute despair, she began an expedition of hope. Her decision to seek the fountain was not without anxiety. However, there was a spiritual element within her that made it possible. She was guided by a deep desire to know how she could find meaning and purpose in her life. Uncertainty and the unknown were frightening, but her need to search for meaning, and heartfelt love, was stronger than her fears.

Lily was ready to do some soul-searching and face up to her own limitations—examining all the thoughts she was holding that prevented her from teaming up with the spirit of love and thanksgiving.

> Tony turned to the audience. Let me share with you that the day I first dived into the unknown... I was afraid, really afraid! However, I eventually became aware that I had been wrong all along... I didn't fear the unknown. What I feared was to let go of the known—losing what I held so deeply in my heart—the mastery of my life under my own terms.

At the station, Lily noticed there were many cities to which she could go and several trains about to leave with different destinations. Which train should she take? To which city should she go? Without knowing exactly where she was heading, she got on the first train leaving town.

The day was beautiful when she arrived in Knowledge City. The sun shining upon the earth and the scarlet bougainvillea displayed everywhere on the walls of the city like a bright quilt, appeared to be whispering 'Welcome Lily.'

Lily sighed. Her heart was pounding faster than normal in anticipation of what she was going to discover in this place.

Knowledge City was a portion of the land which contained an abundance of wisdom. It was a divine place! Lily felt as if she were inside the pages of a fable. She walked in the forest, appreciating the evergreen trees that blanketed huge slopes in the mountain range. Lily closed her eyes to breathe in the clean air.

Lily thought	This feels *good!*
Tony	She sat under a tree to admire the beauty that surrounded her. Suddenly, she observed a dark green trolley coming up the hill toward her. The driver was very nice looking. He radiated serenity. 'Good morning, miss. May I help you?' he asked.
Lily	I hope you can. My name is Lily, and I am searching for the fountain with the water to quench my soul's thirst.
Tony	The driver said, 'It's nice to meet you, Lily. My name is Forgiveness. I know where to find the fountain. Get in... let's have a talk.'
	Lily got in. Forgiveness made her feel comfortable. The trolley began to descend the hill. Lily was fascinated with the view. On the right side, she could see the high mountains standing motionless and unaffected by the environment. They were so high that they seemed to become one with the heavens. To her left, she had a breathtaking view of the turquoise ocean and waves crashing on a sandy beach. The seagulls flew above the water, waiting for the right moment to catch a fish. In the distance she could watch the seals at play. Lily sighed again. It was such a beautiful place!
Forgiveness	I know where you can find the water you are searching for.
Lily	Do you really? Tell me! Where is it?
Forgiveness	It is in the fountain.
Tony	Lily experienced frustration with his answer. She already knew that!
Lily thought	Isn't that what I just said? What I want to know is where to find it!
Tony	Forgiveness noticed her reaction.
Forgiveness	You will get there. There is no question about it, but you are a long way from it.
Lily	What do you mean?

Forgiveness	You see, if you find the fountain you will find rest for your soul. To find such rest is not so easy.
Lily	And why is that?
Forgiveness	It is because in order to find the rest of your soul, you need wisdom.
Lily	How can I find wisdom?
Forgiveness	You find it along the way. You have to walk the path that has been placed in front of you so that you can learn lessons from experiences in your life. It is through these experiences that you will find the wisdom you need. It will prepare you so that you may reach the place where you can be stripped of your worst enemy.
Lily	I don't understand. *Who* is my worst enemy? She frowned.
Forgiveness	It is you! It is you!
Lily	*Me?* Why do you say that?
Forgiveness	You, like most people, are filled with negative thoughts. I can assure you, Lily, thoughts can steer you in the wrong direction. They can make you believe that your life or your circumstances are worse than they are. Also, you harbor hard feelings toward some people in your life and even against yourself. You hold on to resentment and guilt. Let me tell you, Lily, before you can find the spiritual waters, you need to learn to let go.
Lily	What do you mean?
Forgiveness	In order to find the rest for your soul, you need to learn to forgive yourself and others!
Tony	Forgiveness knew Lily was carrying around the baggage of grudges, resentment, and guilt in her heart—mighty obstacles in her path preventing her progress.
	I understand what Lily was going through, because at one time I had allowed that same baggage in my heart and in my mind for a long, long time, and as a result, I hurt too. But one day, a piece of wisdom came to me through my mentor Keith, whom I mentioned before. He said to me:
Keith	Tony, your pain is a result of an error of thought, which can cause severe problems in your life and to your health. Think about it!
Tony	I did think about it and kept it in mind for some time. After a while, I realized that my unhappiness, stress,

anger and the conflict I carried within were caused by my own thoughts and beliefs. He also said 'You can change your thoughts if you keep your inner eyes open... gaining awareness of your wrong thinking...' Over time, I came to the realization that unhappiness is the result of distorted thoughts about who I truly am.

Forgiveness   Lily, if you persist in harboring this rubbish in your heart, it will hold you back in a place of pain, frustration, and despair. Do you understand?

Tony   Lily didn't answer. She maintained her silence. She knew Forgiveness was correct, and she couldn't deny she had hatred in her heart.

Lily thought   But I have my reasons!

Forgiveness   Lily, listen to me. Attachment to stuff like anger and guilt will always hide the truth from you. They draw boundaries and set limits on how happy and joyful you can be.

Tony   A tear ran down her cheek. Lily was angry and resentful because she felt unloved and rejected. All she wanted was to be left alone and not to be compared with others. She wanted to be accepted with her virtues and her flaws and to be loved—loved just the way she was.

Tony looked around at the audience solemnly and said: It's clear that Lily had not yet realized that what she ultimately wanted was to experience the unconditional love that can only be found in the heart of the fountain.

Forgiveness   There are many roads you must take before you can reach the fountain. Every road will teach you a new lesson. If you put into practice what you learn, you will get closer and closer to the fountain. But you have to keep in mind, Lily, that you must take one step at a time.

Lily   What do you mean by 'one step at a time?'

Forgiveness   When you learn a lesson and you put into practice what you have learned, you take a step.

Tony   Forgiveness became quiet as he fixed his eyes on her.

Forgiveness   Lily, I don't wish to impose on you, but the truth is that in order to find the water to satisfy your thirsty soul, you need me. It's necessary to make me a part of your life. You have to want to open the door of your heart to me.

Lily thought   Easier said than done!

Tony	Lily felt so much rage thinking about the people who had hurt her soul so badly. Even though she had tried to forgive and forget, she hadn't been able.
Lily	But, ah .... Forgiveness, she said fumbling, I have at times tried to open the door of my heart to you, but I haven't been able to let you in. Believe me, if I could, I would! But I can't.
Forgiveness	I know you can't. You can't do it alone. Lily, listen to me. As you get closer and closer to the fountain, the source of wisdom and knowledge, strength and power, you will be able to open the door of your heart to me. I guarantee that! You need to find wisdom in your life. Wisdom will help you open your heart to let go of feelings that cause you pain and replace them with joy.
Lily	But... where do I find wisdom?
Forgiveness	I already told you. It is along the way. It is in your life experiences, good or bad. It is in your decisions and attitude.
Lily	What exactly do you mean?
Forgiveness	When you realize the harm you cause to yourself by sheltering corruptions such as grudges, resentment, guilt, jealousy, anger, envy, greed, haughtiness and pride, you will choose to change. That decision will transform you inside and enable you to find the key that opens the door. It is a change in perception. But remember, Lily, the transformation only takes place when you are ready to choose, not before.
Tony	Lily was angry. She did not want to wait for wisdom. The pain was too great.
Lily thought	But I want the transformation now! Right now!
Tony	Sadly, transformation just doesn't work that way. In the matters of the spirit, we have to experience a profound change of heart, and we can't take shortcuts to get there. We have to walk one step at a time and apply to our lives what we learn along the way. Forgiveness continued driving around the suburbs of the city, when suddenly, the trolley made a sharp turn. Lily was ecstatic to see the beautiful view. In front of her were three majestic volcanoes standing on the banks of a clean and peaceful lake. It was a magnificent sight! The clouds covered most of the top of the volcanoes, except for the peaks that managed to escape from the haze. The multi-colored bougainvillea growing down the walls of nearby homes

seemed even brighter, offering a special touch of beauty to Lily.

Forgiveness

I don't know your life story, Lily, ... or against whom you are holding a grudge, or why you feel guilty... but let me share with you a couple of stories that I think will help you. Not too long ago, a man called Richard came to this town. He was filled with anger toward his father. Richard's father, Martin, was not a wise man, and on many occasions he had been verbally abusive. Martin had had an unhappy childhood himself, as his mother had been quite nasty to him growing up. As a result, Martin just didn't know how to be a good father, but he meant well.

Richard, being just a small boy, couldn't comprehend why his father acted the way he did. Richard had a strong personality—even as a toddler—and Martin just didn't know how to deal with him. Martin compared Richard with other children and verbally punished Richard for being strong-willed. Richard certainly didn't feel Martin's love. On the contrary, Martin tried to demand that Richard be sweet and obedient. Richard, however, at the time, was rebellious and willful. Richard longed for affection from Martin. He ached to spend time together, however Martin never seemed to have time for him, and was quite often in a bad mood, yelling and complaining whenever they were together.

Richard felt uncared for and believed he was unworthy of love. It was his belief that his father damaged his heart and affections very deeply.

Richard and I talked for a long time. I tried my best to make him realize that the anger he held onto so tightly was more damaging to him than to his father. 'Richard, you must find the way to forgive your father. You cannot continue carrying such feelings of hatred. Let go of anger and resentment,' I said. 'I can't,' he answered. I looked at him with concern. 'You don't need to forgive his behavior. You just need to forgive him.' I replied. 'I don't understand,' he responded. 'Well,' I proceeded, 'you have legitimate reasons to justify your resentment, but the price you're paying for anger to rule over you is too great. Richard, to forgive doesn't mean that you accept what Martin did to you. No! What it means is that you are willing to make the choice to forgive. It means you no longer wish to carry the pain and sorrow that Martin's inability to love caused you. When you hold hatred in your heart, Richard, you are punishing yourself more than you punish others.'

Tony

Lily was listening, deep in thought.

Forgiveness

Now, let me tell you about Margaret. Margaret carried a great deal of guilt in her heart. She had made several mistakes in her life because of lack of knowledge and understanding. She was devoid of love and short of patience. She thought about herself first, second and third. Based on the standards of the world, Margaret was selfish. Whether those standards were right or wrong, Margaret herself viewed her selfishness as a flaw. She was not fond of herself and didn't accept her shortcomings. Margaret was not proud of who she was, causing guilt to creep all the way into her very being. 'Margaret,' I told her, 'you must understand that whatever mistakes you have made in your life are done. There is nothing you can do to retract them. Whatever is done is done. All you can do is to learn from those mistakes and do your best not to make them again. If you do slip up and repeat past mistakes, don't keep punishing yourself for it. Learn to love yourself and be kinder to yourself and others. You'll find that it's easier to do once you realize that it's your own thinking that creates the guilt in the first place. Your thoughts, and no one else's, keep you in bondage. Everything you do in your life, Margaret, is by choice. You are free to choose anew with each decision. If you made the wrong choice in the past, you don't have to allow that choice to continue making you feel guilty. If something about yourself does not feel right to you, you can choose to change it. You need not live the rest of your life banging your head against the wall because of the errors you have made. You can choose to be the person you want to be. You need to forgive yourself for not being perfect. You will never be perfect, Margaret. Never! But you can reach for excellence. Whatever that might mean to you as an individual.'

Do you understand, Lily? Can you see how important it is to forgive? I am essential so that you can be healed and be at peace. Forgiving yourself first and others next, is the best way to heal a heart. Allow me to flow into you like a waterfall, washing away all the poison of miserable and painful reminiscences. My clean, fresh water will restore your thoughts and beliefs.

Every human being has a work to carry on within,
duties to perform abroad, influence to exert, which are peculiarly his,
and which no conscience but his own can teach.

William Ellery Channing

Tony

Forgiveness and Lily traveled around the city for a few more hours taking in the beauty and harmony of the land. On display were rolling hills, gentle woodlands, flowering fields and sparkling lakes. When they reached the crowded center of town, they could see that many other thirsty souls were also here on a quest for the wisdom that the inhabitants of Knowledge City offered to its guests.

When they walked along the streets, Lily felt as though she had been carried back to an earlier, more peaceful time in history as she strolled its ancient streets and dark alleys. The city had spectacular architecture and large central plazas. Outdoor markets displayed an array of colorful fruits and vegetables.

Forgiveness greeted a lady coming the other way and stepped away to talk to her. They spoke together for a while, and Lily observed them. The lady appeared strong and strict, yet radiated gentleness. At one point they both glanced towards at Lily, so she guessed they were talking about her. During her visit, it became clear to Lily that the goal of the inhabitants of Knowledge City is to help their guests find the answers they need on their quest for the fountain. The residents all live in total harmony, supporting each other, in order to accomplish this task.

They walked towards Lily.

Forgiveness

Lilly, I'd like you to meet my friend. I've told her about your search for the fountain.

Tony

The lady gazed intently at Lily. Without hesitating, she said, 'Before you can be in the position to open the door of your heart to Forgiveness, or to anyone else for that matter, you need to know me. My name is Responsibility, and I am very important in the search of the fountain.'

Responsibility

You see, without me, you can't move forward. You need to make me a part of your daily life and take me wherever you go. Let me explain something to you, Lily. You have misunderstood the meaning of my name. When you think of me, you only relate to me with a sense of obligation, which is only one part of me. But Lily, I am much more than that. I am also the one who will help you have a response to the circumstances of your life.

You must understand that when you live outside of the fountain, your life is in your own hands. Let me say it again: *it is in your own hands*, Lily. Now, let me ask you, what good can that be without direction? You don't even know where you are coming from or where you are headed?

Lily   Nobody knows that! Surely, life is a mystery?

Responsibility   You are absolutely right, Lily. Nobody knows, except for the fountain. That is why you are lost without it. Those who have been able to go beyond logic and reason have been able to make the connection with the fountain. The source of their creation and the source of all wisdom and knowledge is in the fountain. There you will also find hidden treasures that reveal to you the truth, and as a result, your existence will no longer be a mystery to you.

Lily   Could you please explain what you are saying?

Responsibility   What I am telling you, my dear, is that when you live without the awareness that the fountain is in your heart—in your very soul—then you go through life without direction and guidance, hoping that plans you have made by yourself, will turn out okay. If you have not learned to hear the voice of the fountain, you cannot be guided. All you can hear is the echo of your logic and reasoning, the whisperings of fear, insecurity, and uncertainty, along with the murmurs of beliefs imposed on you by the world. That is why it's so important to be one with the fountain. You'll never be able to hear the fountain's voice with a mind that is obstructed with fear, dread and self-righteousness.

Tony   The still and sweet voice of the fountain can only be heard in the spirit.

Responsibility   Let me tell you again Lily, without the fountain you will continue to feel alone and lost—swallowed up by anxieties.

Lily   But, Ah... I know many people who are satisfied with their lives, who rely on themselves alone.

Responsibility   Lily, darling, you don't know people's hearts. How can you know if they are satisfied or not? I agree that some people *think* they don't need the fountain in their lives, but Lily, you do! Don't waste any more valuable time thinking about other people's lives. Think about your own life. You have a choice, Lily. Choose what's best for you based on the needs of your own heart.

Tony	Responsibility looked at Lily intensely.
Responsibility	Everything that has happened to you until now has been your responsibility. Yours, Lily! All your actions and thoughts have contributed to the heaviness of your heart. Your lack of vision has created your circumstances. If you wish to find the fountain, you must accept responsibility, and the sooner, the better! You must realize your life's path has been the result of your behavior, your conduct, your choices, and lack of understanding. Don't feel bad, Lily. I am not saying this to make you feel guilty. I'm just trying to show you that your heart is guided by an authentic need for the fountain, and only when you respond to what it needs will you find rest and tranquility. If you really want forgiveness to come into your heart, you must accept responsibility for the present state of your life. It will help you to stop blaming others for your lack of happiness.
Tony	Lily was quietly thinking this through.
Lily thought	But I haven't done anything wrong. It's not my fault, *they* did it to *me*.
Responsibility	Tell me, Lily. Do you blame others for your heavy heart? If so, you are getting something out of blaming others for your sadness, aren't you? You don't have to answer; *I know*. People always get something out of everything they do, until they come to realize the harsh realities of life and are awakened by the sharp pain and sorrow dwelling within their souls.
Tony	Lily didn't respond; she just wanted to weep. She was finally becoming aware of the cruel thoughts she had been carrying around. She had never felt any personal responsibility for the pain she was feeling. On the contrary, others had inflicted the pain upon her, and *she* was the victim. In her life, she had grown up feeling that the love she experienced had always been conditional and could evaporate at any moment. They had demanded that she be different—to be someone she was not. They had demanded that she be good—and that meant behaving in a way defined for her by others and their expectations.
Responsibility	Look, Lily, she said in a soft tone of voice. One of the most difficult lessons in life is to accept responsibility. When you stop being the victim or the martyr, you leave behind a feeling that unconsciously has brought you pleasure.

Lily	Excuse me? It has brought me pleasure, you say? Do you think I like being miserable? Why on earth would I choose to be unhappy? What are you referring to?
Responsibility	I am referring to the pleasure that is experienced when someone exhibits the need for attention.
Lily thought	I don't want to call attention to myself. All I want, is to find healing for my grief... nothing else.
Lily	Would you give me an example, please?
Responsibility	Yes, of course. Let me share with you the story of Robert. He had a very angry disposition. He was aggressive, dominating and manipulative. He imposed himself on others, mostly on his own family and some friends. He played mind games, and believe you me he was excellent at it! If his family didn't do what he wanted, he gave them the cold shoulder. That was his way of punishing them for not doing what he demanded. Anyone could see that he had a huge problem, but he couldn't see it himself. He was unaware that unconsciously this was his method for calling attention to himself. He liked to be praised and to be noticed. Robert demanded to be Number One in the lives of his loved ones. He felt insecure, and time and time again demanded that they prove their love to him. All the same, their attention resulted in a hollow kind of pleasure that only temporarily filled the void in him.

One day, I called his attention to this behavior—trying to make him understand that he was out of line. He looked at me with rage. 'Why are you getting so angry?' I asked. 'Am I not telling you the truth?' Robert got very, very defensive. 'This is who I am, and whoever loves me has to accept me just as I am,' he answered with arrogance. 'No, Robert,' I said, 'people don't respond well to that kind of behavior. When you make demands, people will turn their backs on you because they don't know how to handle it. When you act obnoxiously, you make them feel uncomfortable. It is a lot easier for them to stay away from you or to fight back, and then you wind up alone. Are you aware,' I asked him, 'that the aggressiveness and the manipulation that you force on others is not actually the essence of who you really are?' Robert looked at me, not knowing how to reply. So I proceeded. 'It is not your real being. It is only the way you choose to carry on. That can be changed, if you so desire.' After a while, Robert came to realize I was correct. He accepted that his angry disposition was the reason why he had been rejected all his life. He understood that his manipulation was suffocating the people he loved most. It was then that he chose to change. When he accepted responsibility for the circumstances in his life, he began to move forward towards the fountain.

On the other hand, Lily, you have to be careful not to accept responsibility that does not belong to you.

Lily	What do you mean?
Responsibility	What I'm saying is that you don't need to take responsibility for the decisions other people make. Everyone has the freedom of choice.
Lily	I don't understand. Please clarify.
Responsibility	Lily, the key here is that you have no control as to how other people respond to their circumstances. The only power you have is how you respond to your own circumstances.
Lily	May I have an example?
Responsibility	Of course you may! Laurie carried a heavy burden because she felt obligated to make her mother happy. Laurie's mother was a hard woman to please. She, Mildred, was a very snooty, know-it-all kind of person. Laurie never got anywhere trying to earn her approval. Mildred imposed herself on Laurie, dictating what had to be done. Don't misunderstand. Mildred was always available for Laurie. She was a great mother as long as Laurie behaved the way Mildred thought she should. I felt for Laurie, because whenever Mildred got angry—which was quite often—the tantrum lasted for several days. The intention, of course, was to keep Laurie under her control and inflict guilt. I was concerned for Laurie. She was a terrific girl who loved Mildred so much. But Mildred's behavior left a lot to be desired. 'Laurie,' I said, 'you must free yourself from the manipulation Mildred imposes on you. Darling, it is not your responsibility to make your mother happy. You can't! Happiness comes from within and Mildred has to dive in and find it for herself. You can't discover it for her.' Laurie looked at me with tears in her eyes. 'I know,' she said, 'but it is so difficult.' I held Laurie in my arms. 'You have to start somewhere,' I said. 'As long as you enable Mildred in her weaknesses, you're not helping her at all. It is not your responsibility to help others see the light, but it is your responsibility to find the light for yourself.'
Tony	Lily was very attentive.
Lily	I understand... I have been in Laurie's place.

Responsibility Let me share another case with you. Josephine believed that she had to live in accordance with the expectations that she thought other people had of her... She pressured herself into thinking that if she didn't act as was expected, she wouldn't be loved. She truly believed she had to be the way other people wanted her to be, or else... shame, shame, shame.

Tony Can you believe it? Can you see what a burden she was carrying? Josephine's mind was troubled. She didn't know that love cannot come from exterior forces; love can only come from within.

Responsibility Josephine had a daughter, Alice. Alice had messed up her life, time and again, with bad choices. Josephine was trying to take responsibility for the decisions and actions that Alice had made. Because Josephine was lacking wisdom and knowledge, she felt guilty if she didn't help provide for Alice's needs. 'That is what a good mother should do,' she recited to herself repeatedly. 'If I would have done this or that, things would have turned out differently.' Josephine caused herself to be under a lot of stress and pressure, thinking that she should be a problem-solver, protector, and source of happiness for her desperate daughter. During one of our many conversations, I said, 'Josephine, you must free yourself from all those expectations that you place on yourself, as well as expectations placed on you by others. Listen carefully. You must not continue trying to please everyone.' Josephine was definitely a people-pleaser. I tried to explain to her that she had to learn to let go of those false beliefs. They didn't reflect the truth and were holding her captive. Josephine's problem was that she needed people's approval.

Tony One of the many issues I had to learn in my life was to overcome my intense need for people's approval. It isn't an easy lesson to accept. We've all heard that we will never be able to please all the people, all the time! It is just not possible. We all are very different from one another. Each one of us has different points of view and values. Even though I still struggle sometimes with my desire for approval, my life is a lot easier when I keep focus on the fact that I will never be able to please everyone. I tell myself 'it's okay, we don't all have to agree... all we need to do is respect each other's uniqueness and individuality.' Seeing it from this point of view helps me respond more positively when someone disagrees with my opinions or ideas. To realize that my well-being no longer depends on people's approval has given me a sense of freedom, and it has unshackled a large portion of my inner being.

Lily was listening very attentively.

| Lily thought | I can relate to Josephine in so many ways... |

| Tony | There were lots of moments when Lily found herself trying to please others. |

| Lily thought | I am weary... I want to be free of all that baggage! |

| Tony | Lily had reached a point where she found herself wanting to take care of herself for her sake, not for others. |

| Lily thought | But, oh my God, if I do that, what are they all going to think of me? 'Shame, shame.... She's so self-centered!' |

| Tony | Lily realized that other people's expectations were causing her intensive pain. It was just too much pressure. |

| Lily thought | Please, someone help me! |

| Tony | She was pleading from the depths of her soul. |

In the fullness of time Lily will understand that there is no problem in wanting to please someone else. It's only a problem when we try too hard because of guilt, or in order to be loved, accepted, or needed. When we act out of such motives, we put ourselves in shackles that can cripple us. However, when we please others with no strings attached, that's a different story. When we are doing it for the pleasure it brings to our own hearts, it's freeing. If only we could understand that, we would live happier lives.

| Responsibility | After a while Josephine learned to be accountable for her own actions and decisions. She understood that even though she had made several mistakes with Alice, the past was just that—the past. She had done the best she knew, good or bad. Whatever was done was done. If she had known better, she would have done better. Therefore, she learned to forgive herself for all the mistakes she made and allowed Alice to walk her own path and learn her own lessons. Thereafter, Josephine was free to love Alice. She could help Alice without the burden of obligation and guilt. She understood that her beloved Alice had to try out her own wings. Josephine had shifted her relationship with her beloved Alice to a place that supported both of them in their journeys. |

| Tony | Responsibility got very quiet. |

Responsibility	Lily, are you willing to be responsible for your own actions and decisions? Are you willing to be accountable for what you have contributed to your own misery?
Tony	Lily did not answer. She was thinking it over.
Lily thought	How did I contribute to my own pain?
Tony	She was trying to weigh up if all those destructive feelings she'd been storing up for years were worth keeping. If only she could just let go of them, then perhaps the pain would go, too.
Lily thought	But surely, I'm not really the source of my own misery? I can see where Josephine went wrong... but me? No. No, no, no. I don't think so!
Responsibility	I understand what you're going through.
Tony	Responsibility looked straight into Lily's eyes.
Responsibility	Lily, I must stress to you how important I am in the search of the fountain. It is imperative that you accept responsibility for your actions, and if you are blaming yourself for the decisions of others, give it up! Every person has choices. You can't choose for anyone but yourself. Choose, Lily. Choose to change your life by becoming accountable for your thinking. Keep in mind that without me, Responsibility, you cannot move forward. I am the second road.
Lily	If you are the second road, which is the first?
Responsibility	Willingness is the first road! If you are not willing to be accountable, you will stay the same.
Tony	I discovered that when my expectations weren't met, I blamed the results on other people. This thinking became second nature to me. It helped me justify that others were responsible for my problems. I realized that my tendency to blame others for my anger, frustration, depression, stress, and unhappiness was holding me back. I had actually chosen to create most of those feelings for myself and certainly couldn't attain peace while blaming others.

You may be deceived if you trust too much,
but you will live in torment if you don't trust enough.

Frank Crane

Tony	Lily was in a deep sleep until the sunshine filtering through the bay window woke her. The rays brushed the beautiful violets on the windowsill. Lily got up and got ready to meet more of the inhabitants of Knowledge City.
Lily thought	I wonder what else I can learn today?
Tony	As she went through the front door, she wasn't paying attention and bumped into someone.
Lily	I am sorry, sir, she said apologetically.
Tony	'Think nothing of it,' he responded, looking at her with surprise. He didn't remember ever seeing her before. 'Are you new in town?'
Lily	Yes, I just arrived and am searching for the fountain.
	'I am happy for you,' he said. 'It is at the fountain where many find the water to quench the thirst of their soul and the answers to the mysteries of life. I have met people who have come here from far and wide looking for the fountain. Some of them have found answers in order to move forward. I hope you do too. My name is Trust. I'm glad you are here. *Welcome!'*
Lily	Thank you, Trust! My name is Lily.
Trust	It's a pleasure to meet you, Lily. Would you join me for a cup of coffee?
Tony	Lily did not feel threatened by Trust... On the contrary.
Lily	I would love to! She answered enthusiastically.
Tony	They walked together toward the outskirts of town, talking as if they were longtime friends. Lily felt so comfortable with Trust's company that even the rays of the sun appeared to be smiling at her. They found a charming coffee shop and chose to sit at one of the tables in the corner by a window. They needed a quiet place where they could talk, but Lily—gazing outside—almost got lost in the view: a rushing waterfall that appeared to split the majestic mountain in two, with its waters falling and splashing into a raging river. The sun peeked from behind a wall of clouds. Its rays reached down and danced on the blue water. Violin music filled the coffee

shop with The Blue Danube by Strauss... and Lily felt immersed in the sweet sound.

Truly, a sweet dose of music and a beautiful view can soothe an aching heart.

Lily	I have heard about you, Trust.
Trust	What have you heard?
Lily	That you are essential in the lives of all human beings.
Trust	Correct... I am essential because I give you a sense of security and a feeling of certainty. You need those to courageously face situations, people, and challenges that you find along the path. My presence in your heart, Lily, is vital, because without me you are not complete.
Lily	How can I trust after my experiences of rejection and betrayal?
Trust	You can only trust—truly trust—when you connect to your inner being and gain the understanding that you really don't trust anyone. What you actually trust is your own judgment and your prejudiced ideas about people. Before you can trust people, you must learn to trust the wisdom and knowledge that are found in the fountain.

Last year, George came to visit. Just like you, George was searching for the connection. George didn't confide in anyone. He felt lonely and afraid. One time when we were chatting, I told him, 'George, I can tell that because of some experiences in your life, you have lost me.' George didn't answer. He was quiet, but his eyes revealed a great deal of pain. I felt so bad for him! He was really hurting because he lacked my presence in his life. I didn't live in his sorrow-filled heart. 'It is very important that I be part of your life,' I told him. 'You need to learn to trust again. Without me, life can make you feel angry, hurt, or discouraged. In other words, without me, you see life through the eyes of bitterness, insecurity, and fear.' George finally spoke. 'You're right,' he said. 'I lost you a long, long time ago.' 'How did you lose me?' I queried. 'I lost you when someone lied to me and took advantage of me, when I was judged and harshly criticized, when I was rejected and made to believe something that wasn't true.'

I felt for George! His heart hurt so much. It was so painful for him to think about confiding in someone and then to be so let down. 'I understand how you feel,' I said, 'but, do you realize, George, that at times, you have done the same thing to others?' I added without expecting an answer. 'If you learn to trust again, you will feel much better.' George just looked at me and then he asked, 'How can I trust again in those people who have hurt me so deeply?' 'Oh, George,' I declared. 'There is your problem! You expect too much from others. If you put your faith and trust in people, you will be disappointed.' 'Why is that?' he asked. 'Your expectations are not realistic. You are expecting your family and friends to be the water that quenches the thirst of your soul. You will never find it there—never!'

Lily, I saw George just look down. I spotted a tear that was trying to escape from the depths of his soul. He didn't want to admit it, but I knew he was longing to have me in his life again. He just didn't know how to open the door to me. 'Look, George,' I said, 'you must know that everyone has limitations, including you. Don't expect people to be the way you want. People will only give what they want to give. If you have had a difference with someone, you need to be willing to resolve the problem. The problem is in you—in your mind. Also, it is important to look inside and accept responsibility for your contribution to the problem. If the other person is not receptive to your efforts, let it go. All you can do is your best to amend the situation. On the other hand, for others to believe in you,' I proceeded, 'you have to keep your word. If you tell a friend, a family member, or anyone else for that matter, that you will do something, do it! Don't use excuses not to follow through. It is a wonderful feeling when people believe in you, however, only if you keep your word will they be able to trust you!

Tony	Trust looked at Lily.
Trust	Lily, can you relate to George?
Lily	*Are you kidding?* Of course I relate to George.
Trust	If you are willing, think about what I just told you. It applies to you as well.
Tony	Trust looked at the time. He had to go.
Trust	I must leave. It was a pleasure talking to you, Lily. I hope to run into you again.
Lily	The pleasure was mine, but before you leave, tell me how one can truly trust? How can one forgive and forget?
Trust	I already told you, Lily. The day you are able to connect with your inner being, you will discover the wisdom to help you achieve whatever it is that you desire.

Lily   But how can one connect with the inner being?

Trust   It takes time. The desire increases powerfully as you get closer to the fountain. First, you need willingness to practice lessons learned along the way. It is through these lessons, Lily, that you will be able to find understanding, knowledge, and insight. That's what wisdom is all about. Wisdom will help you see the inner being and hear the inner voice. Wisdom can be acquired through the experiences of your life and the needs of your heart.

Tony   Trust departed. Lily stayed a little bit longer thinking about their conversation. She reflected on the past. Many people came to mind: friends that had disappointed her, boyfriends who had rejected her, teachers who had verbally abused her, people who had made fun of her, and parents who had demanded that she be different. Oh! It still hurt so much, even though plenty of time had elapsed since the incidents. Lily was still perturbed by the many things that had happened to her.

> What Lily didn't realize yet was that these painful experiences were precisely what caused her to wish for the fountain. One day, she will realize that everything has a purpose in life, and only when the heart has a deep wound does the soul search for shelter. When it finds such refuge, it finds a priceless treasure!

Trust's words rang in her head. 'Do you realize that you have done the same to others?'

Lily thought back to all those people she had hurt along the way: friends she had disappointed; boyfriends she had rejected; teachers she had talked back to; people she had made fun of; and parents she had demanded be different. Trust was right; she had done the same to others. Now she could see it clearly. She also thought about all those promises made to others and to herself that she had not fulfilled.

> When I look back on my life, I remember a time when I said to a dear one, 'How could you let me down when I trusted you so much?' Then as my level of awareness and understanding increased, I found myself wondering if I really did trust that person? I didn't. What I trusted was my own estimation of him. When I realized that my judgment was erroneous, I didn't want to accept it. I did not want to admit that I had made a mistake. I had hoped that he would behave according to my own expectations. But I was wrong; it was a lot easier to blame it on him than on my poor judgment.

Teach me to feel another's woe, to hide the fault I see;
That mercy I to other show, that mercy show to me.

Alexander Pope

Tony

Lily left the coffee shop and as she walked alone, she contemplated all she had been learning. For the first time in her life she craved solitude.

Only in solitude, can one begin to pull out the choking weeds and let the good seeds grow.

After a while, she encountered a charming park and felt compelled to take a stroll there. The branches of the trees were entangled and touching the benches. Sweet alyssum with clusters of tiny lavender, blooming everywhere, announced the arrival of spring. To her right was a sparkling lake with docked sailboats. Its waters were calm and the air smelled clean.

As Lily sat alone, absentmindedly gazing toward heaven, she thought about what else she needed to overcome. While reflecting on her past detours, she was interrupted by the sight of a woman crying on a gentleman's shoulder. Lily wondered why the woman wept. She stayed close by, hoping to eavesdrop.

The gentleman smiled at Lily. 'My companion is crying because she feels sad for that man over there...' he said pointing to his left. Lily turned around to look. She saw a man lying on the ground with a bottle in his hand.

The crying woman looked up at Lily. 'People are so thirsty for the living waters,' she said tearfully. 'They choose to use crutches to help them fill the emptiness of their hearts... even if it is only temporary.' The woman continued crying with such sorrow that Lily's heart was touched.

'What is your name?' asked Lily.

'Mercy,' she answered.

Lily

It's nice to meet you, Mercy. My name is Lily.

Tony

Mercy dried her tears with the hem of her dress. She attempted to smile at Lily.

Mercy

Please don't mind my tears. I just can't help grieving for those frightened souls who don't know how to find the living waters to quench the thirst of their spirits.

Tony

No one noticed another man standing nearby, listening to their conversation. His name was Benjamin. Benjamin typically acted like someone who was totally conceited. While he looked with disdain at the man lying on the ground, he said: 'I, myself, feel empty at times, but I am not in the same dilemma. Weak people—that's what they are—allowing themselves to be inebriated with addictions. It serves them right!'

One day Keith said to me solemnly:

Keith

Tony, don't look down your nose at the alcoholics and drug addicts. Everyone, even you, is addicted to something. People with heavy addictions feel alone, with no place to rest their hearts and souls, so to speak. The awful orgies—alcohol, drugs, and immorality—are like the tentacles of a mighty octopus. They snatch and draw many into their embrace, leaving them adrift, without an anchor to save them from their destruction.

Tony

The gentleman who had been consoling Mercy looked at Benjamin with pity. There is no doubt that judgment and arrogance live in the heart of this man, he thought.

He addressed Benjamin in a soft, gentle tone of voice. 'Sir, you must be very thankful that you are not in the same situation.' Benjamin didn't know how to reply to the gentleman's words. He was a haughty man who looked down on others. Whether he acknowledged it or not, he had an angry heart and was always ready to retaliate. Benjamin was not familiar with this manner of kindness. How could he? He was judgmental and egotistical.

Lily was just standing there observing. She didn't dare speak.

"My name is Humility," said the gentleman tenderly. "What's yours?"

'Benjamin,' he sniffed.

Humility

Let me tell you, Benjamin, with all due respect, the truth is that your attitude is detrimental. You have no right to judge others, my friend. You have no idea what is going on in the hearts of other people. Don't judge. For just as you judge, criticize, and condemn others, it will be done unto you.

Mercy

I agree. Instead of judging others, count your blessings, Benjamin. Have compassion for those who are less fortunate than you. You don't know the sorrow and pain that people carry within. You don't know the reasons why they do what they do. If you did, you might have compassion.

Tony	To understand compassion, we must put ourselves in someone else's shoes and see things from their perspective. When we envision someone else's circumstances as our own, we can appreciate what we have in our lives and we can experience a sense of gratitude.
	Humility looked directly into Benjamin's eyes.
Humility	Benjamin, do you believe yourself to be perfect?
Benjamin	No, not perfect, but at least *I* have willpower.
Humility	...and just because you have willpower you feel that you have the right to point your finger at others?
Tony	Benjamin did not respond.
Humility	My dear Benjamin, one of the most difficult lessons in life is to learn not to judge others. Probably everyone has heard the warning that the same way you judge others, you will be judged.
Benjamin	But people have always judged me! So, what difference does it make? he said angrily.
Humility	It makes a big difference. When a man doesn't judge, he is less likely to mind if he is judged. But, when he judges the way you do, he lives wondering what people are saying behind his back, and believe you me, that wondering causes a lot of oppression.
Mercy	Yes, that's a fact. But as I already told you, try your best to see people with a little more compassion. Not everyone is as fortunate as you.
Humility	That's right. Instead of judging, seek to rectify your own faults. Don't think of yourself better than them just because you have willpower. Benjamin, willpower is simply a tool. Treasure it! I sincerely hope you never lose it.
	Mercy, it's time to go!
Tony	They cordially said good-bye to Benjamin and Lily. Benjamin left without saying a word.
	Lily stayed there thinking and admitting to herself that she had been guilty of exercising judgment on others.
	Lily understood that she had no right to pick on people, attack their failures, or criticize their faults. She had heard Humility say that judgment has a way of rebounding. Lily didn't want to experience that. She could see only too clearly

her own faults and failures, and promised herself she would do her best to refrain from judging others in the future.

One of the most frustrating experiences in my own life is when I lack understanding regarding other people's behavior and choices. It is very tempting to pass judgment on them. Sometimes, I am bothered by what seems to be illogical, unreasonable, foolish, crazy, ridiculous, absurd or irrational behavior. I am discovering that I am almost always the one who is acting unreasonably. It is absurd of me to expect that others be, and act, the way I think they should. People do crazy things. So do I. We all do! The way I see it now, it's me who needs change. I need to not get so bothered or upset by people's behavior and choices. After all, it's really none of my business.

> ***Peace is such a precious jewel that I would give anything for it but truth.***
>
> *Matthew Henry*

Tony	The sun began to set. The rays painted the scenery in the most beautiful colors. Lily was ecstatic observing such splendor. She stopped to admire the exquisiteness of nature, and all it offers to those who are open to see it. Single colors appeared to be entangled and united without boundaries.
Lily thought	What a majestic creation!
Tony	Lily was silent, attentive and delighted with the stunning view. For a brief moment, she forgot about all her sorrow and stood there in utter amazement.
	An elderly woman was observing her. Lily could feel the stare and turned to see who was watching. When their eyes met, she felt a special magnetism. There was something distinctive about the woman. She looked so calm, as if she had no worries or concerns. There she was, just sitting tranquilly watching Lily. Lily approached the bench and the elderly woman looked at her with loving eyes. The woman asked, 'May I help you?'
Lily	Well, um... I just want to meet you. There is something about you. I don't know what it is, but I feel so wonderful in your presence. Please forgive my boldness, but the truth is that you intrigue me. Who are you? 'My name is Peace,' she answered.

Lily	Where do you live, Peace?
Peace	I live in the fountain.
Tony	Lily could not believe what she was hearing.
Lily	In the fountain? she shouted with excitement.
Peace	Yes, in the fountain.
Lily	Oh, Peace, I have come from very far away searching for the fountain. Will you please tell me where it is?
Peace	Yes, my dear, the fountain is within you!
Lily	The fountain is within me? I don't understand how that can be.
Peace	Everyone has the fountain within, but most people do not realize it. They keep looking for it outside themselves. People are thirsty but they don't know how to tap into the free-flowing water. It is just lack of knowledge. But if you really want to find the fountain, you will. It is just a matter of time and willingness. You'll find it. I promise you.
Lily	How do you know I will find it? Lily was curious.
Peace	Because, the fountain has placed a desire in your heart to be filled with its living waters—and when you discover the fountain, I myself will live in you. I must go now.
Tony	She stood and started walking away from the bench.
Lily	Wait, wait a minute! Could you come and live in me now? pleaded Lily. Pl-e-e-e-ease?
Tony	Peace turned around.
Peace	My dear, she said, overcome with sorrow for Lily, I can't, but I will, eventually. First, you need to learn to forgive, trust and be kind to yourself and others. I cannot live in your heart otherwise.
Lily	Why not? That's an awful lot to ask.
Peace	It is because you entertain thieves that rob you of my presence in your life. You will never experience me in your heart as long as you hold ill feelings and hatred toward other people and yourself. Let me tell you something else, most people don't live their lives to the fullest.
Lily	Why don't they?
Peace	People walk through life as if they were dead. Do you realize how very short life is, Lily? It can come to an end sooner

than you expect. Therefore, be fervent in whatever you do. It's time to live, so live, and when it's time to die, die.

Lily thought | That is precisely why I am searching for the fountain, so that I may live.

Peace | Give yourself more freely to others, Lily. When you give, you also receive. We receive in proportion to what we give. When you give freely you experience tranquility and satisfaction within, which in turn will allow my existence in your heart.

Tony | Peace affectionately patted Lily's back and smiled tenderly.

Peace | Do not dismay, my dear. Keep on searching. Follow the paths. Learn the lessons. Put into practice what you've learned. Listen. Listen. Listen and be accountable. If you do, you will find the way. I promise you that!

Tony | Peace then walked away. Lily felt a greater thirst. She knew it was imperative to find the fountain.

Lily thought | Peace said that she lives in the fountain.

Tony | Lily knew she could not live without peace, and she was determined to acquire it.

It brings to mind those days when I continually postponed experiencing peace in my life. I didn't do it on purpose, though. I just thought—like most of us—that I would be at peace when all the things I wanted were attained. In the meantime, my life kept moving on and peace was not a part of it. Peace came into my heart when I was willing to settle the score with the world and stop struggling against the natural flow of life. When I tried to change the things I could not change, I kept peace away from me. But now I know that to have a life filled with peace, the endeavor must start within me. No one can provide the peace I desire for me. Only I can find it, as I grow closer to the fountain, the source of all the things my heart desires.

It is better to have loved and lost,
than to not have loved at all.

Alfred Lord Tennyson

Tony | Lily sat on the bench engrossed with the beautiful sunset. It filled her soul with the tranquility of the evening. She stood up and walked toward the panoramic view of the canyon behind her. Vehicles were coming up to the summit of the mountain, driving along a road that snaked through the huge red rocks. There was a mystical hush in the air.

Lily spent several hours indulging in the gorgeous surroundings. Her imagination moved like a roller coaster as she tried to take in the incredible red rock formations. As evening came, the sky was so clear that the stars looked like fireworks frozen in place in the sky. Venus, the evening star, was the most brilliant of them all, and a beautiful orange full moon illuminated the earth. Lily walked towards the restaurant located on the seashore. There was a gentle wind blowing. She chose to sit at one of the tables outside and let the ocean breeze caress her face. Lily noticed an older gentleman sitting behind her. She took note of how well he was dressed. He was very, very handsome. The gentleman smiled at her with a great deal of charm. Lily couldn't explain the wonderful feeling his smile instilled.

'Good evening, miss,' he said. 'My name is Love'.

When Lily heard his name, she stopped in her tracks.

Lily thought	Did he say 'Love'? Is he the same love that has been eluding me forever?
Love	What brings you here?
Lily	The fountain, she said abruptly. I am in search of the fountain.
Lily thought	...not that YOU care.
Love	May I sit with you?
Lily thought	Better be careful, Lily... Love hurts too much. Remember your pain? He caused it!
Lily	Honestly... I'd rather you wouldn't.
Love	Do I frighten you?
Tony	Lily felt awkward.
Lily thought	I just mustn't give in! He will hurt me again if I do.
Lily	No, you don't frighten me. I just don't want anything to do with you.
Love	May I ask why not?
Lily	You hurt me! she snapped, looking at him angrily.

Tony	Love looked at her with such a tender gaze that Lily's heart softened. Lily didn't want to admit it, but she felt so much joy in his presence. He radiated such a wonderful feeling.
Love	Why are you in search of the fountain?
Lily	Well... um... because I am too tired of feeling empty.
Lily thought	...tired of running after *you*.
Lily	My soul is very hungry, and I know there is a special place where I belong. I believe that only the waters of the fountain can fill me up.
Love	What does finding the fountain mean to you?
Lily	It means finding knowledge and wisdom. I need them so I can break down barriers that have been chocking me with pain and sorrow for so long.
Tony	Love took Lily's hand.
Love	Lily, the fountain is within you.
Lily	Yes, that is what Peace told me. She also says she abides in the fountain.
Love	Yes, as do I!
Lily	You do? *No! I don't believe that!*
Love	Yes, Lily, I do!
Tony	Lily was blind. She couldn't believe that love lived in her heart, because she had never experienced it.
	Ladies and gentlemen, I believe what all of us need is the experience of Love. Pure Love.
Lily	But Love, if you and Peace live in the fountain and the fountain lives in me, then why am I so miserable? Why am I so troubled? Why have you eluded me?
Love	I have never eluded you, Lily. The truth is that you have looked for me in the wrong places.
Lily thought	Looked in the *wrong places*? Yeah, right!
Lily	What does that mean, 'the wrong places?'
Love	You have been expecting me to come to you through a special person or friends or family. They are the channels of love but they are not the source of love, Lily.
Lily	Who is the source of love, then?

Love	The fountain is! You are miserable because you haven't learned to listen to the voice of the fountain—your inner voice. For the same reason, you lack forgiveness and trust in your heart. You need to learn to hear the whisper of the voice abiding within you, Lily. That whisper will reveal the truth to you.
Lily	How come other people find you in their lives, through the channels, I mean. I don't even have that, she said with bitterness.
Love	Yes, you do, Lily. You have a lot of me in your life.
Lily	No, I don't, Lily retorted with misty eyes.
Tony	Reflecting on her lonely life nearly caused the tears to spill. She definitely did not want to burst into tears in front of Love.
Lily thought	I need to end this conversation... it's bringing back way too many sad memories for me...
Tony	Love knew that something inside Lily was obstructing his presence in her heart.
Love	Are you talking about romantic love, Lily?
Lily	Well, yeah, she answered, biting her lips to keep from crying. *Everyone* needs someone special in their life!
Love	Ah, now we're talking! replied Love with a charming smile. What people need is pure love, Lily. The world has made you believe you can only be happy and complete if you have someone special to love you. That is a misconception.

If you are relying on a person to make you feel complete by taking away loneliness, you are going to be very disappointed. As your illusions about love begin to crumble, you'll begin to see that human company does not erase loneliness. Loneliness is obliterated by pure love that emanates from the fountain within you. Very few find the love that is available to all. It is a love that can fill all the voids. You are looking for romantic love because you believe a romance will fill the void, and it would, to a certain extent. But the kind of love your heart desires, Lily, can only be found inside of you. The day will come when you will awaken inside. Then you will be joyful. You will be filled with overflowing love, Lily. When you find the fountain, your heart will be so satisfied that you will look back at your life and realize that if you had to experience the pain all over again in order to find the fountain, you would. I promise you that.

Lily thought	There is no way that I will be willing to go through all that pain again! Who is he kidding?
Love	There is a season for everything, Lily, and everyone has to experience their own awakening. You are encountering yours!
Tony	Love could see all the negative feelings residing in Lily's heart. They were powerful adversaries. Their job was to stop love and peace from abiding in Lily's soul. Lily needed to know this; she needed to understand it, and she was going to—at a later time.
Love	When you learn to open the door of your heart to forgiveness and trust, you will experience my presence as well as peace. Look... we already abide in your heart, because that's where the fountain is and we live in it. But all the false beliefs you hold on to, stop you from experiencing our presence in your life.
Lily	I see, said Lily, feeling heaviness. I have a question. How can I learn to open my heart's door to forgiveness?
Love	One way would be by accepting responsibility for the results you have in your life. Responsibility is a major road to the fountain.
Lily	How can you say that the fountain lives in me? I wouldn't be looking for it if it lived in me! Could you explain that?
Love	Sure, Lily. The fountain lives at the center of your heart. But you have buried it under layers and layers of fear, insecurity, resentment, pride, arrogance and more. Ambitions have made you blind to your own needs and to the needs of those who are a part of your life.

Lily, before you can tap into the source that can quench your thirst, you need to realize that those feelings and those imperfections keep you away from the fountain—from the truth. You must be willing to choose to change—to see it in another way. Then the fountain, which is already abiding in you, will be able to bring forth goodness.

It is only when you walk the path placed in front of you, seeing with the eyes of the Spirit that your experiences—good or bad—become your lessons. You will recognize that those lessons are precisely what will supply you with the wisdom you need to see and understand.

Lily	Wisdom to see and understand what?
Love	What the fountain is all about.
Tony	Love looked at Lily with such warmth in his eyes.
Love	Lily, right now, during your search, you are attending the university of the Spirit. One day you will obtain your master's degree in wisdom. Wisdom will help you connect with the fountain. When you learn and understand that the fountain lives within you, you'll discover that you can become one with it. Practice the lessons that you have been taught along the way. Everything works one step at a time. Don't rush things, Lily. You will get there when the time is right for you, but know that you are already in the flow. Now, I must go...
Tony	Love stood up. He embraced her tenderly. Lily wished this moment could last forever.
Lily thought	Don't go, please. Don't go. Stay with me forever!
Tony	Love looked into Lily's eyes so deeply that it brought tears of joy. Love just smiled and whispered in her ear.
Love	Lily, the fountain lives within you and will never leave. But you are not conscious of its presence. You will be, Lily, because you desire it with all your heart. The fountain will indeed bring you to a higher level of experience and revelation—to a higher consciousness—because there is such a need in your soul for its living waters.
Tony	Love began to walk away, and he turned around to look at Lily one more time. He smiled at her. She was so dear to him, like everyone else was. Lily was sad to see him go. She saw something unusual in his eyes—something distinctive— but she couldn't tell what it was.

Love's eyes were saying, 'Oh, my child, how precious you are to me. When you are ready, Lily, you will understand that the fountain and I are the same. Do not be entangled in the things of the world, for they are brief and impermanent. Love is what rules the spiritual world. Without me, you are nothing. Nothing! You will come back to me, darling, in the fullness of time.'

Lily was alone again. From the deepest part of her soul, she cried. It was going to be so hard to trust and forgive. She was not ready to accept responsibility. She had lived all her life blaming others for her sadness and pain. Now, she had been told to find wisdom. Where was wisdom?

Lily thought

Oh my, the matters of the Spirit are not easy tasks! But aren't Peace and Love worth it? Didn't they say they live in the fountain?

Tony

I can relate to Lily. I had the same kind of thirst. When the moment came for me to recognize the abundant life that forgiveness, responsibility, trust, mercy, humility, peace and love could bring to my life, I decided to continue searching until I could possess those jewels. After a time, I understood that love is what makes life worthwhile. Now I know that the sweetness of love cannot be discovered if I keep looking outside of myself. If I do, I will fall for the wrong thought that a special person is the source of my love. Real love does not need any person. Love lives in our hearts. We experience it to the degree in which we allow it to flow. I was drowning in what society calls love, but I found myself lost and lonely because I didn't meet the world's standards of love and those standards certainly didn't meet mine. Now I understand that what our culture calls love, is not love at all.

Tony paused. One day I asked myself. 'How can love evolve into a desire to control and possess someone?' That sounds more like manipulation and codependence, and that, certainly is not love. Where there is love, there are no demands or expectations, and no dependency. Love means freedom. Pure love, with no strings attached, allows one to be free to love and be loved. Real love springs forth from inside.

Lily had acquired a lot of information in Knowledge City— facts and bits of wisdom to help her throw off the gray blanket of grief and sorrow wrapped around her soul. Lily was eager to continue with her journey and wanted to learn more.

Now the question was: Would Lily apply what she was learning? Was she willing to take action and stop feeling sorry for herself?

I suggest that we all seriously consider what Responsibility said: 'Without willingness it is impossible to choose to make a difference in one's life.'

Lily went to the station to take the next train. She got in and sat by the window. Not knowing the destination, she only hoped it was the city where she could find wisdom. On her way, she thought about the wise friends she had just met in

Knowledge City. She made a mental recollection of their teachings.

Lily thought Forgiveness told me that when I am unwilling to forgive, I am only punishing myself. I didn't realize it before, but it makes sense now.

Responsibility said that without her I will not move forward toward the fountain. I will not be able to advance as long as I keep the belief that someone else inflicted my pain.

Trust told me how essential his presence is in order to enjoy a sense of completeness.

The advice Mercy gave Benjamin was to see people with compassion. 'Not everyone is as fortunate as you,' she had told him.

Humility said to refrain from judging and criticizing, because I will be judged with the same yardstick. Ouch! That is a tough one. I will keep it in mind; I certainly don't want people to judge me.

Peace said that the fountain lives within human beings, but as long as I harbor so many flaws, I won't be able to experience its presence. Oh, no! I desire to experience the presence of Peace in my heart. That's for sure! I will find the way. I will. I have to!

Love told me that I need to learn to listen to the still, small voice of truth. He advised me to find wisdom. Wisdom will help me unite with the fountain. Love also said that he lives in the fountain and the fountain lives in me. Therefore, he lives in my heart, but I am not yet aware of his presence. Most importantly, he said that he never eluded me and he waits to fill my whole being. I sure hope so!

Tony Lily was serious regarding her search for the living waters. She was willing to follow the advice of these wise friends. She closed her eyes, looked within her heart, and took a good look at her life. She allowed herself to be honest and could see that, yes, she had been a major contributor to both her past and her current situation.

Lily thought Responsibility is correct. I have made a big mess of my life and I am willing to accept it. Enough is enough. It is time to stop blaming others for my lack of happiness.

Tony

Lily thought about her broken relationships. Her lack of understanding had at times made her overreact; blow things out of proportion; hold on too tightly; and focus on the negative aspects of her life... causing her much heartache. To her surprise, she noticed that her heart already felt lighter. Lily actually felt a sense of relief. When she accepted responsibility for the results of her life, calm washed over her. A heavy load was removed from her shoulders; a veil had fallen off her eyes. Lily smiled!

> It is my belief that Lily began to discover the hidden treasure when she was able to see what most of us cannot—that if she accepted responsibility for the circumstances of her life, she could get rid of all those feelings that kept her in bondage. As long as we allow those emotions to live in our hearts, we will live oppressed by their dominion, making us feel miserable. I know I have experienced what it means to live under the authority of bitterness and discontent. You probably know it too. We all experience those emotions at one time or another. Ladies and gentlemen, to learn to accept responsibility for our actions is one of the greatest treasures one can find, because it helps us to set ourselves free from many burdens.

Chapter Three: Flesh City

There are two freedoms – the false, where a man is free to do what he likes; the true, when a man is free to do what he ought.

Charles Kingsley

Tony

Lily let out a deep sigh. She began to enjoy the new feeling of relief. She was finally experiencing freedom. She thought about those times when anger had gotten the best of her. Oh! What an awful feeling anger was. It had been in her heart for so long. It had made her so miserable and hurt her soul so deeply. So very deeply!

Lily was very thankful to have found a way to begin eliminating anger and resentment. She knew it wasn't going to be easy, but it was going to be worth it. She knew there was a way to free herself up from the hold that destructive feelings and thoughts had over her. She recognized now that she had a choice in how she responded to life.

Lily looked through the window, observing the brilliant, jewel-like colors of fall trees. The leaves were vividly alive with glowing reds, ambers and yellows. It was a glorious feast for her eyes. The leaves appeared to be dancing to the rhythm of the wind's symphony. The birds flew in formation, one behind the other in total harmony as they started their journey south. The sound of the river running alongside the road was keeping her company. The majestic mountains appeared to be smiling down at her. They invited her to delight in their splendor. The jolt of the train interrupted her thoughts. She had arrived at her next stop.

Nightfall had descended. Lily took her luggage and walked toward the exit. She noticed the flashing sign above the entrance of the station. WELCOME TO FLESH CITY. At the door was a very handsome man. He welcomed the passengers with a hard-to-resist, seductive smile.

'Good evening, miss. Welcome to Flesh City! My name is Temptation.'

Lily

Good evening, Temptation, said Lily, unable to take her eyes off him.

Tony	Something about Temptation attracted her greatly, and she felt captivated by his smile. Lily tried to hide the thrill she felt.
Lily	Temptation, could you please tell me, where could I find wisdom?
Temptation	Wisdom, you said? He squinted at her.
Lily	Yes, I have come from far away looking for wisdom. I was told that I might find it here.
Temptation	Why are you looking for wisdom?
Lily	Oh, Temptation, I have a thirsty soul! I know that wisdom can help me get in touch with the fountain where there is water to quench the thirst of my spirit.
Tony	Temptation laughed raucously until his eyes were full of tears. He placed an arm on Lily's shoulder.
Temptation	Miss, you have come to the right place. It sounds to me like your soul is thirsty for the pleasures of the flesh. If you stick with me, you will be in good company.
Lily	What do you mean?
Temptation	Miss, here in Flesh City, you will meet several of my favorite guests. They will gladly help you quench your thirst. I promise! he said with a hard to resist smile.
Lily	Is that so?
Temptation	Yes, miss, I guarantee you'll have the time of your life here!
Lily	Well then, thank you, Temptation. I look forward to meeting your friends. As she left through the door, Temptation winked at her.
Tony	The city was bright with flashing neon lights everywhere, promising a good time to its guests. Lily was tired. She needed to rest. She entered the first hotel she found. At the counter was a woman who, even though she seemed nice and caring, looked rather serious.
	'Good evening,' she said with a kind but firm tone of voice. 'My name is Conscience. May I help you?'
Lily	Thank you, Conscience. My name is Lily. I would like a room, please.
Conscience	Sure, for how many nights?

Lily	I am not sure. I am looking for something and don't know how long it will take. By any chance do you know where I might find wisdom?
Tony	Conscience looked thoughtful, and without blinking an eye said,
Conscience	Not *here!* Not in Flesh City!
Lily	Why not?
Conscience	Wisdom doesn't live in Flesh City.
Lily	Where does it live, then?
Conscience	It lives in the City of the Spirit.
Lily	And where is that?
Conscience	It is on the opposite side.
Lily	Is it very far?
Conscience	Oh! Yes. It is completely on the other side of the mountain.
Lily	Can you tell me how to get there?
Conscience	Yes, but before you can get there, you need to go through this town.
Lily	Why?
Conscience	Well, because you will need to make a decision.
Lily	I don't understand!
Conscience	I know, but you will soon.
Tony	Flesh City was a big town. Many of its guests got lost there. In this city there were tons of pleasures. Flesh City offered very tasty foods. The majority of its visitors chose to stay. There was a lot of fun for some, a lot of sorrow for others. That is why Conscience said Lily would have to make a choice. Lily would have to decide if the nourishment Flesh City offered would quench the thirst of her soul, a decision only she could make.

**No one would allow garbage at his table,
but many allow it served into their minds.**

Fulton J. Sheen

Tony	Lily got up early. She took a warm shower while planning her day. She was eager to go to town and explore. She dressed,

grabbed her purse, and went down the stairs, humming a
song. She boarded the city bus heading to the center of town.
The route ran along the coast. The scenery was superb. Lily
noticed how the waves separated themselves from the vast
ocean, rolling in, rushing and smashing against the rocks on
the shore.

> In my earlier life, I was walking alone in this world,
> separated from my Creator, tackling by myself the
> obstacles that I found on the path. Tony shivered.

Lily continued observing the vast ocean. On the horizon the
ocean appeared to become one with the sky. Elsewhere, she
could make out boats with frogmen who were preparing to
plunge into the ocean's depths, excited about what they
might discover.

> Ladies and gentlemen, let me share something with you,
> if I may. Several years ago, Keith, my mentor, told me:

Keith	Tony, if you wish to discover what dwells in the center of the fountain, you have to be willing to dive into its very core. You must first submerge, drink, and bathe in its pure and clean waters.
Tony	The bus arrived at the center of the city. Lily walked to the pedestrian area. Temptation was standing in the shadows, chatting with someone who obviously was a good friend. Lily felt nervous. Temptation noticed her and he clearly remembered seeing her at the station. He looked at her with an intense, seductive gaze.
Temptation	Good morning, miss. Are you having a good time?
Lily	Well, no, not yet. I just arrived.
Tony	Temptation didn't take his eyes off her... smiling and showing his perfect white teeth.
Temptation	May I ask your name?
Lily	It's Lily.
Temptation	It's nice to see you again, Lily. I'd like to introduce you to a very good friend of mine. This is Pleasure.
Lily	Nice to meet you, Pleasure.
Pleasure	The honor is all mine!
Tony	Temptation turned to Pleasure.
Temptation	Let's escort Lily around our city and show her a wonderful time while she is with us. I would love for her to decide to

stay and live with us forever. Lily has a thirsty soul. Will you help me fill it up?

Pleasure Of course. You can certainly count on me.

Tony Pleasure was no less charming than Temptation. Lily was captivated by both of them. They made her feel good. To a point, they even filled the emptiness of her heart, even if it was only temporary.

Over the next few hours, Pleasure and Temptation worked overtime to show Lily a tour of Flesh City. Lily felt drawn to these beings and even seriously thought about staying. Pleasure and Temptation spent a great deal of time with her. They did their best to gradually hook Lily into seeking her happiness through the desires of the flesh.

Tony They did the same to me. I became a slave of their charm, ensnared by their tentacles.

Temptation Lily, we will be right back. We have to attend to some business. But please, make yourself at home. Remember, you are in Flesh City, the city of pleasure and fun. It's a chance to let your desires run wild. You only live once; enjoy yourself!

Tony Have you ever wondered, if you were absolutely free to do as you wish, would you truly be happy and at peace? Many of us seek complete freedom to act as we desire. We want to be free of all restraints, somehow believing that if we could do just as we please, this will bring us happiness and peace. Why then, are lonely feelings residing in the hearts of so many who indulge themselves?

'Be careful,' said a gentleman standing close to Lily. Surprised, Lily turned around and stared at him. I beg your pardon? 'Be careful,' he repeated. 'If you are not careful, they will destroy you!'

Lily I am sorry, but I don't understand what you are talking about.

Tony 'Let me introduce myself. My name is Self-Control and I have come to warn you.'

Lily My name is Lily, and I don't understand why you are warning me.

Self-control Look over there, he directed, pointing to the nearest restaurant. It is lunchtime... Pleasure and Temptation want to give all their guests the best. Do you know what their best means, Lily?

Lily	I suppose it's to have fun and provide delight.
Self-control	Let me show you the price people pay for these delights. Look at those people in the restaurant, especially the overweight man sitting by the window. His name is Douglas. Douglas has a compulsive eating disorder. He is addicted to food. There are plenty of others with addictions to drinking, smoking, drugs, shopping, work, sex, etc. But let's focus on Douglas.
Tony	Lily looked in that direction. Douglas was carrying a lot of weight. Lily noticed that Douglas walked toward the center of the room. He seemed to be having a difficult time moving, yet he walked in the direction of the table that was abundantly displayed with every imaginable kind of food.
Self-control	Douglas thinks he is in heaven. He loves to eat. Everything tastes so incredibly good to him. Watch him closely, Lily. He eats, and eats, until he is stuffed. Do you know why he does that?
Lily	Probably because he enjoys food?
Self-control	No, Lily. It is one thing to enjoy food and quite another to use it to try to fill the emptiness of the soul. Douglas is abusing food to temporarily forget his thirst. What do you think Douglas needs?
Lily	What?
Self-control	Love! He is starving for love in his life. Come with me.
Tony	Self-Control and Lily entered the restaurant at the precise moment that Pleasure and Temptation were talking to Douglas.
	'Are you enjoying the food, Douglas?' they asked in unison.
Douglas	Oh, yes, he answered with his mouth full, shoving in another bite. It is wonderful, he declared while crumbs of bread fell from his mouth.
Self-control	Sadly, Douglas is not telling the truth, Lily. Deep within, he feels awful—controlled by the desires of the flesh.
Temptation	We are glad you're pleased, Douglas, this is just one of many things we can offer in this city. Later on, we will introduce you to Indulgence, who will take you for a ride! She is a very close friend of many inhabitants of Flesh City.
Tony	Self-Control made eye-contact with Lily.

Self-control	Indulgence is excellent at deceiving people. She will shackle them with heavy chains and take over as their idol and master, a ruling force over them.
Tony	Lily was listening intently. Self-Control and Lily sat down at a table.
Self-control	Watch, he directed.
Tony	Lily noticed that Temptation and Pleasure were sitting next to Douglas, waiting for him to feel better after such a feast. Pleasure motioned to a couple of his best friends
Pleasure	Douglas, he gushed, allow me to introduce Gluttony and Lust. We all work together to satisfy our residents. They want to keep you company while you are here. You'll get attached to them. I promise!
Tony	Lily stared at Gluttony and Lust. They were not appealing to the eyes. Gluttony looked disgusting as he smiled at Douglas. Lust looked even worse. Saliva dripped from his mouth, full of crooked, yellow teeth. Lily felt repulsed. Self-Control seemed distraught. It was painful for him to see Douglas in such a predicament.
Lily	Are you all right?
Self-control	Well, I have been better, he replied sadly.
Lily	What's wrong?
Self-control	Douglas! You see, Lily, now Douglas is captivated by Pleasure, Temptation, Indulgence, Gluttony, and Lust. He enjoys their company because they make him feel good, for the moment. Douglas refuses—he is blind—to realize that he is out of control. These beings dominate his will; he is powerless. They are so captivating, and Douglas is enamored. At this stage of his journey, it is easier for Douglas to satisfy the thirst of his soul, by gorging with food than to seek healing of his addiction.
Tony	Self-Control quietly thought about what he was going to say next.
Self-control	Douglas is not taking responsibility for himself. If he continues allowing his new companions to rule his life, he will regret it.
Lily	But, he can't help it, surely. Those beings have become powerful and prominent in his life. The grip of fleshy pleasures is unbelievably strong and causes poor judgment.

Self-control	Precisely, and that's because he's ignoring the inner voice shouting that there is a way to overcome the demons in control of his will. He is reasoning, analyzing, and trying to justify staying in Flesh City. He is hooked! His mind is telling him that he is strong enough to deal with the enticements of Flesh City, but he isn't. Lily, they will only magnify the void in his heart and emptiness of his soul.
Tony	Lily didn't say anything. She knew in her heart that Self-Control was correct; she couldn't argue with the truth.
Lily	I thought pleasure was important in life. Are we not to have pleasure?
Self-control	Pleasure is not a bad companion. He won't harm you as long as you don't allow him to mingle with Indulgence, Gluttony, and Lust. Their influence is so powerful that when they work together, you'll fall on your knees and worship them. Therefore, you must be very, very careful!
Tony	Lily understood what Self-Control was talking about. She had her own demons. Just like Douglas, she had given them authority over her life. Lily had tried—over and over again— to fight their magnetic power, but she had not been able to resist them.
	Lily couldn't conquer her demons because she lacked the strength and awareness found in the fountain. She needed the liberty and power of the fountain to overcome these beings and rise above them. The more she relied on her own strength to defy her demons, the stronger they grew to be.
	I know this to be true, because I experienced it. The harder I tried to change something in my life, the worse it became. The more I resisted something, the greater power I gave to it. I talked to Keith and he assured me:
Keith	Tony, when you focus on your demons, you empower them. You won't win by fighting but by turning on the inner light, and then, their dominion over you will melt away.

Pure motives will make clear flame.
Impure motives are the smoke that clogs the flame.

Sidney Cook

Tony	Lily was walking in the woods. It was getting dark, but the fireflies came out in a display of remarkable blinking lights.

The river in front of her was running freely. Lily wanted to put her hand in the water and let it run through her fingers. Even with the little light coming from the moon and fireflies, the water sparkled. Lily stood on the banks of the river watching the flitting lightshow. She was contemplative— thinking about the demons that inhabited her and how difficult it was to allow Self-Control to rule over her desires. Just like most people she knew, she delighted herself in the fleshly pleasures, but the price was higher than what she was willing to pay. That was one reason she was so desperately searching to connect with the inner source of strength and power.

Footsteps interrupted her concentration. Lily stood up straighter. Her heart was beating so hard that she could feel the vibrations in her ears. 'Good evening, miss. It's a beautiful evening, isn't it?' said a voice somewhere behind her. Lily's voice came out barely a whisper. She cleared her throat and tried again.

Lily	Good evening, sir, she replied looking at him in disbelief. His head had two faces, which frightened her.
Tony	'Don't be afraid. I don't intend to cause you any harm,' he assured. Lily relaxed a bit, but just couldn't take her eyes away from how he looked.
Lily	What is your name? she dared to ask.
Tony	'My name is Success. What's yours?'
Lily	Lily, she answered, unable to stop staring.
Success	It's a pleasure meeting you, Lily, he spoke politely. Are you surprised by my two faces?
Lily	Well, since you mention it, as a matter of fact I am.
Success	Truthfully, Lily, I have many faces, but I will show you only two: one born in the heart of men, and the other springs from their flesh.
Lily	Please explain what you're saying.
Success	When I am a result of the heart Lily, I fill men's souls with joy. When I come from their flesh, I fill their souls with gluttony and greed, which is not the real me!
Lily	I beg your pardon? Lily was aghast.
Success	When people are able to acquire me, I bring so much gladness to their hearts. When someone seeks my presence in his life because he wishes to achieve his absolute best, I

	will live in his heart. If, instead, he seeks me in his life because he believes he is superior to others, I will abide in his flesh.
Lily	Well, I happen to believe that you are necessary in my life. I need to know that I have succeeded in things I've set out to do. This gives me self-worth. I get so disturbed when I don't accomplish my goals. I feel failure, which is not pleasant.
Success	Do you set those goals for yourself or to impress others?
Lily	Excuse me? she said raising an eyebrow.
Success	Do you understand the difference between worth and value, versus dominance and control?
Lily	What do you mean?
Success	Well, let me put it to you this way. When I abide in the heart of a man, Lily, my goal is not to make a man of success but to make a man of value—to become the best that man can be—and my presence follows as a result. Regardless of the interpretation that society has given to my name, if you do your very best in whatever you do, putting your whole heart into it, you are already successful. Always remember this: you can only do so much, but you must strive for excellence in all you do.
Tony	I think we can agree that it is not about perfection, it is about excellence—when we strive for excellence, then we get real progress.
Success	There are those who seek me in their lives just to earn the recognition of others. That does motivates some people to be the best they can be. But I can tell you that the freedom found when you're motivated to do things without one thought for recognition, is priceless.
Lily	I see, she said, still a little skeptical.
Success	Sometimes, people can be deceived by their concept of me.
Lily	What do you mean?
Success	Many people believe that if they have me in their lives, they will automatically be happy. That is not always true, Lily. There are many successful people that have no joy in their lives.
Lily	And, why is that?
Success	It is because their success is based on worldly expectations.
Tony	Lily gazed intently at him.

| Lily | But there are many who have achieved a great deal of power in the world because of their accomplishments... |

Lily

But there are many who have achieved a great deal of power in the world because of their accomplishments...

Success

Indeed, but keep this in mind... When their power comes from within, they will continue to be victorious and successful until the day they take their last breath. But if their power is fed by external sources, it will cease when their abilities are no longer needed. What kind of success do you wish to have for yourself, Lily?

Lily

Well, I wish to succeed in my quest for the fountain. That's what I really long for.

Success

In that case, that's what you must concentrate on. Stay focused!

Usually people wish to obtain me based on worldly standards; they think that will bring happiness. However, the type of success you are searching for will bring you joy. Great joy.

Lily

How can I achieve such success?

Success

You can find it when you follow your heart's desire—or to be exact, when you follow the desire of your soul. Don't compare yourself to other people, Lily. You have to answer only to your own heart. Some people are born to excel in specific areas of life. Others are born to excel in other areas. For some, I am in their hearts. For others, I am in their flesh. Keep striving for your goal of finding the fountain, which is already unearthed at the core of your heart. Reaching that goal will give you an unceasing strength that no one can steal.

Tony

Lily was paying close attention to Success.

Lily thought

So... I have to make my own decisions. It does not matter if I am not as good as the next person; I will be fine as long as I do my very best—that's all that counts. Oh, what a relief to know that I don't have to compete with anyone anymore. I only wish to compete with myself and excel in those areas where I can make a difference. I like that! I believe I can live with that!

Tony

Let me stop right here to share something with you. What a blessed relief it was when I realized that there is no need for me to prove myself to others. Before I arrived at this realization, I felt the need to point out my accomplishments and brag about myself. But now, I know that bragging was nothing but a sign of insecurity.

Keith once said to me:

Keith

Tony, keep your accomplishments to yourself. Most people are not interested in what you have done, or in how much you have. They are more interested in what you have learned, in who you have become. They are most interested in your inner peace. Tony, if you have inner peace, you can enrich their lives. Having a lot of money is not the same thing as being successful. Success means to reach the place in your life where you don't have to apologize to anyone, don't have to explain yourself to others, don't have to spend your energy wondering what other people think or say about you, and where you don't feel you need to control or manipulate others. That is what I call success.

Lily

It is getting late; we'd better get going.

Success

Would you like to go for a walk tomorrow?

Lily

Yes, I would like that very much.

Success

Ok. It's a date, then. I will meet you here. I will bring a friend along. Like me, he has many faces, but once you understand his position in your life, he will bring you much delight. See you tomorrow then.

If you make money your god,
it will plague you like the devil.

G.K. Chesterton

Tony

It was dawn. Lily was awakened by the ferocious sound of a thunderstorm. Torrential rains were pouring down. Lightning bolts were coming down from the sky with so much power that Lily was extremely frightened. She scooted down under the covers, quivering with dread. How small she was next to the forces of nature! She realized that the storm could wipe her and everything else off the face of this earth in a second.

How vulnerable we human beings really are! When we honor our vulnerability, we can draw from within the strength we need, and accept the boundaries and limits of our existence.

Lily kept peeping at the lightning blinking through the blinds. She wished that someday she could also see the light she hungered for—the light to awaken her from the empty life she was living.

The storm began to subside. Lily got up and looked out the window to determine if any harm had been done by the heavy winds She couldn't see any damage. Everything appeared to be fine.

Lily thought	I guess it will be safe to go meet Success.
Tony	Success was standing next to his friend under a weeping willow. His friend also had two faces just as he had warned.
Lily thought	Success sure wasn't joking.
Tony	One face looked very attractive but the other looked like it had a mean streak.
Success	Hi. I am pleased you could make it. That sure was a heavy storm this morning.
Lily	Oh, yes! I was so frightened by the thunderstorm.
Success	I understand that. Those thunderstorms can frighten anyone with their roar like a furious lion. But I am glad you are fine. Lily, I would like you to meet my friend.
	The friend extended his hand and smiled at Lily. It is nice to meet you, Lily. My name is Money.
Lily	Likewise, it is nice to meet a friend of Success.
Tony	The three of them began to walk through the woods. Many trees were down as a result of the storm, and there was mud everywhere.
Success	Come this way. We can walk better on the other side.
Tony	They moved toward their left. The river was running wild, like an unruly child. They sat on a huge rock on the riverbank. The birds were singing in such harmony that they sounded as though they were singing romantically to each other.
Money	Have you heard about me?
Lily	Yes, I have, as a matter of fact, quite often. You are a very powerful being.
Money	Yes, indeed, he replied. Many people adore me because I get them what they want.
Lily	And what they need!
Money	Not always, he said in rebuttal.

Lily	I beg your pardon? she said. She raised her eyebrows.
Money	There are many times when I am not able to give people what they need. There is no question that I do try to provide for their immediate needs, and for some, I provide their wants.
Lily	What are you talking about? You bring so much happiness to people's lives, don't you?
Money	I bring happiness? No, Lily, you are mistaken.
Lily	I am sorry, but I don't understand. I know many people who have you foremost in their lives and they're very happy.
Money	Are they really?
Lily	Yes, they are!
Money	How do you know that?
Lily	I can see it.
Tony	Money just smiled and shook his head.
Money	You cannot see their hearts, Lily. I am telling you, money cannot buy happiness for people. If they are as happy as you say they are, it is not because of me.
Tony	Lily was getting annoyed.
Money	I can help people acquire comfort and achieve recognition, but not obtain happiness. People find the benefits of money irresistible. Because of that, many live their lives chasing after me, trying to possess me. They love me so much, Lily, that some will kill, lie, fight, or cheat for me, and they temporarily lose their way in the process.
Lily	Well, that's going too far! But surely there are also hard-working, honest people who have worked very hard for what they have...
Money	Yes, indeed, but Lily, you are talking about happiness, aren't you? And I am telling you that I do not buy happiness for anyone. I don't have that ability.
Lily	And why don't you? You rule the world!
Money	That's partially correct. I rule the material world. Happiness and joy are not of the material world. They are of the spiritual realm. That is why I cannot help people buy them. Happiness and joy cannot be purchased. I am not the source of happiness. I am not the source of joy. I am only a source of comfort.

Lily	Isn't comfort the same thing as happiness?
Money	No, Lily, it isn't. Happiness and joy are a result of a soul which is at peace. Happiness and joy come from within. Comfort is external. It means possessions or material things. Men can possess happiness and joy even if they have little, but they can never possess happiness and joy just because they have a lot of stuff. I live outside of men, as a part of the material world, and even if men have me in abundance, they can never ever possess the abundance of a spirit that is at peace... because the fear of losing me is always present and there can't be true peace where fear abides. I have two faces, Lily, just like Success. People can be deceived by their concept of me. They believe that they can be happy if they have me in their lives, but that is not always the true. It is an illusion.
Lily	Yes, it is true! I have seen it. As a matter of fact, I have experienced it myself.
Money	The happiness I provide is temporary. It's the type of happiness that men have while I am around, but when I leave, there is nothing left. Money does not build a solid foundation in their souls. Do you understand?
Lily	Are you saying that we have to be *p-o-o-o-o-r* in order to experience happiness and joy? she asked, rolling her eyes.
Money	No, that is not what I am saying. What I am saying is that you cannot rely on me for happiness and joy. I cannot provide them for you. See this other side of me? He pointed at his mean streak, the one Lily had noticed as soon as she saw him. There is this side of me that will break a person's heart. I can be a mean and nasty fellow, Lily. I can leave whenever I want to. No one can tie me up. I am unpredictable and can leave without remorse because, Lily, I have no heart. That is why I am telling you that you cannot rely on me. Can I heal a broken spirit, Lily? No, I can't. You can like me Lily. You can benefit from me. You can even acquire me in abundance and enjoy what I can provide, but don't trust me to provide the needs of your soul. If you do, I will hurt you.
Tony	Lily was quiet. She did not know what to say. She wanted to make sure she understood what she had just heard. She had always believed that money and success were important in life and now after speaking with them, she was a little bit confused. Was she misinterpreting the concept? Success and Money noticed Lily's confusion. Success ventured to clarify things for her.

Success	Lily, we can be good for you. There is no doubt about that.
Money	When people keep company with greed and lust, they can't help being influenced by them eventually. But if my presence is as a result of hard work, dedication and determination, I can be great and wonderful to have around.
Success	There is nothing wrong with having money. To tell you the truth, money is indispensable for comfortable living. Money can buy you many things that will bring pleasure to your life. What is not ideal for you, however, is to be a slave to money and to make it a god.
Money	Let me put it another way: Isn't it strange how many people labor under the delusion that material riches will bring them satisfaction? They imagine that with me they can purchase all the things they want. Now, let me make something crystal clear. There is nothing wrong with me. Some people believe that I am the root of all evil, but it is the love for me—the craving for money and the desire to get me at all costs—that becomes such an obsession and almost a religion with many people. This obsession is what wounds, starves and obscures their soul. There are rich people who live in little bungalows and very poor people who live in mansions on the hill. It is not what you have that brings happiness and joy to your heart and mind. It is who you are. After all, the best things in life cannot be purchased with a coin.
Tony	That reminds me of a tale I heard many years ago about a man who became lost for many days in a forest. Desperate for food and drink he searched and searched. Finally he came across a bag left by someone. With great hope he opened the bag, but was distraught to find there was only money inside. 'They are only coins! They are only coins!' he cried. He had all this treasure in his hands, but it was of absolutely no use to him.
Lily	But Money, how can I tell if I'm in bondage to you?
Money	You are in captivity when you cannot detach yourself from me.
Tony	Each one of us knows in our respective hearts, if we are in bondage to money, and most of us are.
	There was silence. Lily needed some time to assimilate what she had just heard from Money and Success.
Success	You must be careful with us. We can fill your heart with false pride, vanity and arrogance if you aren't on your guard.

Lily thought	Gee, now you're telling me that I am doomed for feeling proud!
Tony	Lily looked them in the eye.
Lily	Are you insinuating that pride is bad? Do you mean to tell me that it is wrong to be proud of what one accomplishes?
Money	No, Lily, don't get confused here. Pride is not bad. False pride is!
Lily	False pride, what's that? Lily was curious. What is the difference?
Money	Pride is that good emotion you experience when you feel good about the things you do and when you reach the goals you have set for yourself and also when you are satisfied with who you are.
Lily thought	Oh, what a relief.
Money	False Pride, on the other hand, is when you consider that you are better than someone else because of what you've done, or when you judge yourself superior because of what you have.
Lily	Oh, now I am in total agreement with you.
Success	Always remember this Lily: It is not what you possess, that should make you proud, but who you have become.
Tony	Money motioned to Lily to come closer and he whispered in her ear.
Money	You do not need me in order to buy a single necessity of the soul, Lily. You don't need me in excess to be happy. Happiness is already a part of you. The problem is that you have been polluted and contaminated by the world. You have been brainwashed with many illusions about the meaning of money and happiness. Listen, you already have happiness. It lives within you, but in order to experience it, you must drop your illusions and the rubbish society taught you about me.
Tony	I remember the days when I used to chase after money. The more I had, the more I wanted, and it was never enough. I will tell you the truth. I was afraid to lose it. Money was all I had, and I couldn't imagine living without it. I was so afraid of not having enough, that I was unable to let go of it. No way! I thought. If I give it away or if I share a little bit with other people who have less than I do, I will not have enough for me, and I held on very tightly, and when I say tightly, I mean tightly. Don't misunderstand me here, I gave money away, but I

always complained about it. I was giving out of fear—duty and obligation—because if I didn't give, guilt showed her nasty face. One day, as my awareness of the fountain—the provider of all things, including money—grew to a higher level of understanding, I was able to discern that I am not here to serve money. On the contrary, money is here to serve me. Ever since I had this revelation, I have been able to depart from the love of money and enjoy it without fear of not having enough. Today I see things differently. I am able to choose to leave the future in God's hands, and have confidence that all my needs will be met.

The only tyrant I accept in this world
is the still voice within

Mahatma Gandhi

Tony	Lily went back to the hotel. She had a lot of thinking to do. She had spent quite a long time in Flesh City and had been shown many lessons. Now she had some homework to do.
	When she went into the hotel, she saw Conscience helping a woman who was sobbing. Jackie was her name. Lily didn't want to disrupt so she quietly went around them. Conscience motioned for her to come closer, so Lily approached them reluctantly.
	Conscience held Jackie in her arms in a most loving way. She held her trembling hands and allowed Jackie to sob as much as she needed to. Lily felt uncomfortable being there since the conversation seemed too personal for her to witness.
Conscience	It is okay, Lily. Jackie is searching for the fountain, too. So you can stay and listen.
Tony	Lily's heart began to beat like a drum in her ears. Jackie and Lily exchanged glances with each other. There was a longing in Jackie's eyes, the same longing that abided in Lily's.
Conscience	Jackie, I would like to tell you something about me. I didn't tell you before because it wasn't the right time. You needed to be ready to listen. Now, I think you are! So, I would like to tell you that I am part of wisdom. Just like Love, Peace, Forgiveness, Trust, Mercy, Humility, Responsibility, and Self-control. I also live in the fountain. Jackie could not believe her ears. 'Don't be afraid, Jackie. Do not dismay. You are not alone. I am with you. Wisdom is waiting for you, too.

The reason for your existence is to find it! You cannot rush things. You have to walk the path that is placed in front of you.'

Tony	Without taking the needed steps, nothing will ever change. Like they say, without the notes, there is no music.
Conscience	I am here to help you make the right choices, to warn you, caution you, speak to you, in your heart.
Tony	Jackie often heard an inner voice speaking to her. She looked at Conscience in disbelief.
Jackie	Do you mean to tell me that it is your voice I have heard inside of me?
Conscience	Yes. I am the voice of wisdom, who speaks to you through me.
Jackie	I don't think I understand.
Conscience	I know you don't understand, Jackie. Understanding comes by revelation. You cannot understand until you see, and to complicate matters for you, you cannot see until you understand.
Jackie	But, Conscience, said Jackie fumbling for words, I want to see and understand. I want to find wisdom. Please help me.
Conscience	It will be my pleasure, Jackie. If you really want to find wisdom, you must be willing to listen and be willing to act. I will help you. But remember, I can only show you the way; it is up to you to walk the path. I can only direct you; it is up to you to follow. I can only tell you where to go; it is up to you to choose to do it. There are many places you must go where you will have experiences and lessons that will help you. Don't be in a rush, Jackie, because the path will only unfold one step at a time. I am with you in your heart. I will speak to you. Listen to me and be willing to act. Always remember that I am the voice of wisdom, at least until you find it inside yourself. When you do, it will speak directly to your heart.
Tony	The sun was shining in through the window, making Jackie's face glow. Something had clicked in her heart, too. She thanked Conscience and walked away with a blissful smile.
Conscience	Lily how was your stay in Flesh City?
Lily	To be quite honest with you, I have mixed feelings. A part of me wants to stay and a part wants to leave.

Conscience	I understand. You want to stay because the pleasures you find in Flesh City are very appealing, very alluring. You wish to leave because those pleasures have become uncontrollable and have an overwhelming power over you. Am I right?
Lily	Yes, you are. I need to get out of here before it's too late.
Conscience	If you were to leave Flesh City, where would you go?
Lily	I would go to the City of the Spirit. Isn't that where you said wisdom abides?
Conscience	Yes, it abides there, but as long as the pleasures of the flesh have the upper hand in your life you won't be able to move to the City of the Spirit.
Lily	How come? asked Lily, feeling discouraged.
Conscience	If you wish to be united with the fountain, you have to learn that you cannot live in both places simultaneously.
Lily	But why not? I don't quite understand. How can I stop experiencing the needs of the flesh? That's the way I was created, with flesh, body and soul, isn't it?
Conscience	It is very simple. If the pleasures of the flesh are governing your life, you cannot apply the wisdom that abides in the fountain. In other words, the flesh and the soul appear to be two enemies. You cannot be a friend to both. You must make up your mind as to which you will abandon and which you will take pleasure in. Do you understand Lily? You cannot have them both. Either you are cold or you are hot. In the matters of the spirit, you cannot be lukewarm. But don't panic, I exist to help you so that you do not succumb to the lures of the flesh. Flesh will always be a part of you. You can't get rid of it, but you can stop being its slave. You are the only one who can make the decision as to whom you belong. I can only speak to you in a whisper. You are the one who decides if you want to follow or not... and if you don't... please know that there is no outside punishment or condemnation in store for you. The only judge is yourself, however you'll simply continue suffering and feeling miserable just like before, until you are ready to choose differently.
Lily	But, ah, that is very tough. I won't deny that I have heard your voice, quite often as a matter of fact. But it is very hard to obey you.
Tony	Yes, indeed. It is very hard when you try to do it by yourself. But when you invite the fountain to help you see things differently, it becomes much, much easier.

Some people believe that to have the freedom of choice means suffering and sacrifice. We hear them say: 'That's what it means to have the burden of choice. It's not easy at all. It is the hardest decision you will have to make in your life.'

These thoughts inflict fear in people's hearts. What we need to know is that if we really wish to connect with the fountain, we can, because the fountain is within each one of us.

On the other hand, we also need to know that whether or not we connect with the fountain, there is no punishment and condemnation. These thoughts about punishment and condemnation give life to guilt. Whenever we are feeling guilty about the power that fleshly pleasures have over us we are giving guilt the upper hand. With guilt ruling over us, we certainly will not be able to experience the fullness and abundance of the fountain, because it is impossible to do so when our flesh is in ascendancy over our spirit.

But don't be alarmed, and let's not forget that it's a process. Let's not feel bad because we are not perfect, but rather let's remind ourselves that at least we are indeed in the perfect place for the next step of our unfoldment.

Conscience	It will take time to get rid of all the baggage you have accumulated in your heart. Those very things drive you to choose the things that Flesh City offers that temporarily fill the emptiness of your soul. The process begins when you catch a glimpse of the source of your creation within you. In other words, when you come in contact with the fountain, you realize that there is power—great power—that can be drawn from it. It's a kind of power that can help you identify those feelings and emotions that are holding you back and driving you to yield to the flesh. When you reach the place in your journey when you can claim—choose—the power of the fountain, your need for inner peace will be filled, and the fight will be won.
Lily	When does that happen?
Conscience	It's already happening.
Lily	How come I don't see it?
Conscience	It's because you are expecting to see results all at once. It doesn't work that way, Lily. You have to go through all the steps so that you may be able to see the whole picture. Don't be afraid or discouraged, Lily. There is one thing I can

	promise. I know who the fountain is and can guarantee that the fountain will see that you get to it.
Lily	What do you mean?
Conscience	The fountain will make it possible for you to choose without so many burdens. You will get to a place, Lily, where you will make choices because you *want* to, not because you *have* to. All you need is to be willing to be made willing.
Lily	I don't quite understand. Who will make me willing if I am willing to be made willing? Lily pondered in wonder.
Conscience	The fountain will. Isn't that promising?
Lily thought	Yes, it is. It is indeed. What a relief! Lily sighed.
Conscience	For now, keep searching. You are getting closer and closer to the fountain. I will tell you the same thing I told Jackie. 'Do not forget that I am with you already, in your heart! I will speak to you. Listen to me and be willing to act.
Lily	Thank you, Conscience.
Tony	Conscience gave her a pat on the shoulder.
Conscience	If you do the best you can Lily, which is all you can do, you will succeed. Guaranteed! Conscience gave a reassuring wink and smiled.

If it were not for hope the heart would break

English Proverb

Tony	Lily went up to her room. Her conversation with Conscience had made her feel better. Calm washed over her. She sat on her bed with her eyes closed and let out a deep sigh. After conversing with Conscience, Lily knew she was not alone. Conscience had said that she would be with her. Nevertheless, Lily felt very fearful. She didn't believe in herself. She did not trust her emotions. They had failed her so many times and now she was faced with the decision to choose to be hot or cold. After giving it long, long consideration, she came to the realization that she was far from making such a choice.
Lily thought	How can I choose? I don't even know who or what the fountain is.
Tony	I can go back to those years when I felt the same way as Lily. I didn't know anything about the fountain. I knew

my failings, and although they were causing me harm, I had become accustomed to them. They brought pleasure to my life, even if it was only for a short period of time. That was better than nothing. But, the fountain, what had the fountain brought me? As far as I could see, it had brought me nothing special. So, the way I saw things back then, I could not choose either, at least not for a long time. But let me tell you, when I came to experience the presence of the fountain in me... Tony's voice broke and a tear ran down his cheek. He cleared his throat and went on. When I came to experience the presence of the fountain, what a change in my life! But, like we have already heard, everything happens in the right season, and every man has to experience his own awakening.

Lily moved towards the sofa to watch television. She didn't want to think about anything anymore. She sat down, feeling so hopeless.

Lily thought	I don't have the inner strength, she sadly admitted.
Tony	She closed her eyes and rested. Lily heard the voice of Conscience speaking in her heart: 'You need Patience, Lily. Patience will help you tremendously. It is not an easy task to find Patience, but when you do, the fruits are sweet. Once you have found her, you can have what you need. Hang in there. You are not alone!'
	After a while, she opened her eyes, but was speechless. A gracious woman was standing in front of her, right there in the middle of the room. She was looking at Lily without speaking. Lily stared back without knowing what to say.
Lily thought	Who is *this*?
Tony	The woman gave her a sweet, pleasant smile. 'Don't be frightened. My name is Hope.' Hope looked fantastic! Lily had to admit that she felt comfortable in Hope's presence. Lily could tell Hope was there to help. She could feel it.
Lily	Hello, Hope. Won't you sit down? Who are you and what are you doing here?
Hope	Forgive me for intruding. To answer your first question, I am your friend. What am I doing here? I am here to carry you.
Lily	Did you say to carry me?
Hope	Yes, Lily, I am here to carry you, she reiterated.
Lily	And just how are you going to do that, Hope?

Hope	I am going to open my arms to you, Lily. My arms are strong and sturdy. You can rest in them. You surely will need them in your search for wisdom.
Tony	Lily's heart was touched.
Lily	Hope, I can tell that you have my best interest at heart. Thank you so much, but could you explain to me exactly what you mean?
Hope	Lily, it is dangerous out there. Without wisdom, you don't know where to go. All you have is what you have learned from other people just like you. You don't know what will happen tomorrow, but wisdom does. It knows everything. My job, Lily, is to carry you while you search for wisdom. Once you find it, it will hold you itself. In other words, Lily, when you find wisdom, you find rest. If you find rest, you have found the fountain. Wisdom and the fountain are one. I believe you have heard before that the reason for your existence is to find wisdom and rest—to reach that special place in your heart where you can hear a sweet and soft voice, lovingly whispering to you that all is well, regardless of the circumstances in your life.
Tony	Lily was about to say something, but all of a sudden, she heard the voice of Conscience saying, 'Be still and listen.'
Hope	I am here to hold you and other souls like yours—souls hungry for the food only wisdom can offer. When you find wisdom in your life, Lily, I will no longer be carrying you, I will be in you.
Lily	What do you mean 'in me?'
Hope	I am part of the fountain and therefore, I live within you, too. But I will remain outside of you until such a day when you come to realize that you don't need to seek me anywhere other than in your own heart. That's where the fountain abides—in the core of your soul.
Tony	Lily looked at Hope with gratefulness in her eyes.
Lily	Thank you, Hope. Thank you very much for being here.
Hope	Don't thank me, Lily. Thank the fountain who sent me.
Tony	Conscience's words came to Lily's mind: 'There is one thing I can promise to you. I know the fountain and I know the fountain will see that you get to it.'
Hope	I will tell you something else. Harmful thoughts are present in you. Stop trying to change what is outside of you. I want

you to know that external circumstances have no power to hurt you, unless you give them power. We all know how much you hurt. You have built thick walls that you hide behind. Learn to stop hiding behind your walls, behind your issues. Those issues are bricks in the wall and can be taken out one at a time. There is a special place for you, Lily, and for everyone else.

Lily

All I want is to find my place in this life, whatever that place might be.

Hope

Don't dismay, said Hope, I have arrived and will not leave you.

Tony

Hope, hope, hope, said Tony sighing. I used to hurt so badly because I didn't allow hope in my life. I didn't want to hope for anything because I was afraid to be disappointed. I had experienced disappointment many times before and knew how much it hurt. I didn't want to experience that pain again. No! Oh no, no, no!

Tony got quiet for a few seconds. He was pacing back and forth.

How awful life can be without any hope. I know. I have been there. However, after a long journey—when I acquired the wisdom and understanding from the fountain—I experienced the other side of the coin, and ever since then it has been possible for me to rest in the tender arms of Hope. Whenever my heart needs to be lifted, I feel Hope gathering me up in her gentle arms of care.

Chapter Four: Relationship City

Be patient with everyone, but above all with yourself.
I mean, do not be disturbed because of your imperfections,
and always rise up bravely from a fall.

St. Francis de Sales

Tony
Lily slept soundly and peacefully after her conversation with Hope. She woke up feeling an unfamiliar sense of relief. The weight on her shoulders was not as heavy as it had been. Hope was helping her carry it!

Lily thought
How good I feel! Now that I have met Hope, I feel like I can continue my journey to that special place where I belong.

Tony
Paying attention to her thoughts and behavior, Lily was eager to continue with her search. She was beginning to tune in to the spiritual world, diving into the unknown.

However, as we watch her go along, she will experience periodic returns of bitterness and anger. Lily will learn from the journey of returns. The day will come when she will be able to master her own self—with the help of the fountain.

She packed her luggage and went downstairs to have coffee and a bagel. She walked to a window table and sat down. Gazing out at the pewter-colored sky, she saw that the mountain summits were now covered with a thin layer of early winter snow. Lily was staring out the window thinking about where to go next. She knew she still had a long way to go before she could reach the fountain, but at least now she had Hope to accompany her.

Lily went to the station to take the next train. She got in and sat at her favorite place—by the window. She had acquired a new insight! She loved to sit by the window to admire and be awed by the world. Some of the magnificent landscapes she had seen along the way had made her reflect on spiritual things. The incredible formations of nature filled her with wonder.

The train was going very fast.

Lily thought	My life is moving very fast too, and I have not yet found the fountain. I have found various drops of water to help extinguish the thirst of my soul though. That's good, I guess...
Tony	The train was snaking through a bustling ski area. The scenery was just glorious. Snow covered the mountain summits, with the sun peeking from behind a mass of clouds. Most of the trees were covered with sparkling white snow, except for a few green branches of pine trees. Everything looked clean and pure.
	Lily's enjoyment came to an abrupt end: Paul and Rita entered the compartment, interrupting her thoughts.
Paul	Excuse us.
Tony	They wanted the empty seats next to Lily. They sat down without even looking at her, or asking if the seats were available.
Lily thought	How rude!
Tony	Lily made no attempt to reach out to them either.
Lily thought	If they are going to be rude and won't talk to me, then I don't want to talk to them!
Tony	She just sat there waiting and expecting Paul and Rita to initiate a conversation. At the same time, Paul and Rita were waiting for Lily to make the first move. Neither one reached out to the other, so the three of them sat together for a long, long time exchanging only glances and not a word.

> It is amazing to realize how little eye contact most of us have, especially with unfamiliar people. I always wondered why, and now I know that it is because we are afraid of each other. We don't trust one another, and consequently we are usually unable to open our hearts to strangers. Truthfully, I had a huge problem reaching out to people. But thank goodness I was able to overcome my fears when I began to think of people as being a little more like myself. I began to smile more often and realized the importance of treating them with kindness and respect—just the way I want to be treated by others. Now, nine out of ten times when I reach out to people, I immediately experience a response. People are waiting for someone to reach out to them, and they—at least most of them—seem to appreciate my effort.

One of Lily's major problems in life was people. She didn't know how to act towards them. Lily did not trust them. She had built all kinds of walls around her to shield her from people's meanness. She didn't allow anyone to pass through those walls. On many occasions, people tried to reach out to Lily, but Lily stopped them from getting close. She was so afraid to be hurt and had made a decision a long time ago that it was a lot easier and safer to keep her distance.

Lily was drinking a soda, and she accidentally dropped the can. Some of the wet, cold liquid spilled out on Paul's lap. He looked at her in rage. 'You idiot,' he thought, but didn't utter a word as he wiped himself off.

Lily	I am so sorry, she said, feeling terrible.
Tony	Paul didn't even acknowledge her.
Lily thought	What a jerk!
Tony	Lily gave Paul a nasty look and allowed feelings of anger to take over, stealing the last of the joy she had been feeling that morning.
Lily thought	People! I hate people!
Tony	She was so irritated that her mind wasn't all that clear. There was a lady sitting in the back of the train observing the situation and shaking her head in kindly disapproval.

By the time the train reached its destination and came to a stop, it was late in the evening. WELCOME TO RELATIONSHIP CITY read the sign above the station's front door. It was a bitterly cold night. Strong winds were blowing snow everywhere. Lily stood up. She looked at Paul and Rita coldly, then grabbed her padded winter coat, scarf and gloves and turned her back on them without saying one word. Needless to say, she was tired and out of sorts. All she wanted to do was to take a hot shower and forget about the whole incident. She was not about to give Paul and Rita another minute of her *precious* time.

Lily thought	They aren't worth it. They are nobody important.
Tony	Lily was upset because Paul and Rita treated her exactly the way she treated others. But Lily could not see, at least not yet, that she usually acted with indifference and little tolerance towards others.

Lily hadn't reached that place within herself where she could see that usually people act in that way because they are carrying open wounds. Because of that, they snap at the first opportunity they have because this helps them to vent some anger. The day will come when Lily will be able to see people differently, with eyes full of love, care and compassion. This is not that day, though.

Lily left the station in search of a place to spend the night. She found a small hotel. It was nothing fancy, just a place to sleep and clean up. She pushed open a tiny door and there it was—a new challenge. She stepped in, not in the mood to talk to anyone.

'Good evening, miss', said the desk clerk. 'May I help you?'

Lily	I would like a room, please.
Tony	Her words were polite, but the tone of her voice betrayed her bad mood.
	'Are you traveling alone, miss?'
Lily	Yes, I am, she answered quickly.
Tony	The attendant asked, How come?
Lily	Excuse me? said Lily, giving him a dirty look.
Tony	'Why are you alone?' repeated the attendant. 'Is that by choice?'
Lily thought	That's none of your business! she fumed.
Tony	Lily ignored him, but her heart didn't. Why was she alone? She didn't think it was by choice, that was for sure, or was it an unconscious choice? She was alone and consequently lonely because she didn't know how to relate to people. She was judgmental of everyone and had high expectations. Her anger made her less than a pleasant person. Even the people she loved the most did not wish to be around her.
Lily	May I have a room, please, she snapped.
Tony	'Yes, miss', said the attendant, noticing that he had upset her. 'I better shut up about anything except a room,' he decided. 'We do not have a room available with a single bed. Would you be interested in one with a double bed?'
Lily	Yeah, yeah, said Lily very impatiently.
Lily thought	This fellow is getting on my nerves!
Tony	She took a double room on the first floor. When she opened the door, she was surprised to find two single beds, and a woman resting in a large rocking chair.

Lily thought	Oh how wonderful!, He gave me the wrong room! How can people be so incompetent?
Lily	I am sorry, said Lily to the lady. I believe I have the wrong room.
Tony	'No, you don't. This is your room, Lily.'
Lily	Do I know you? asked Lily, with a questioning countenance. 'No, unfortunately, you don't, but you will. Come in. Shut the door. My name is Patience, and I have come to rescue you.'
Tony	Lily didn't move.
Lily	You said to rescue me?
Patience	That's right, to rescue you!
Lily	Why would you rescue me? From what? Lily's heart was pounding so hard she felt like it was going to fly out of her body.
Patience	Did you notice your behavior in the train? I was watching you, Patience informed her with a smile.
Tony	Lily didn't know what to say.
Lily thought	Uh, oh. Think fast.
Lily	I don't understand, she ventured.
Patience	You don't understand, Lily, or you don't want to understand? Patience asked in a soft tone of voice.
Tony	Lily didn't know what to say. She was caught off guard. She knew what Patience was referring to. Lily didn't say anything. Embarrassed, she looked at her feet, holding onto the knob of the door. Patience walked towards her, and with a tender motion of her hand, she lifted Lily's chin.
Patience	You don't have to be embarrassed, Lily. All you have to do is to observe—without guilt or condemnation on your part— your own behavior so that you may become aware of how you are relating to others. Do you remember how rude you were to the hotel's desk clerk?
Lily	Well, I'm tired. I wasn't in the mood to talk, answered Lily in distress.
Tony	She closed the door and put her suitcase down by the empty bed.
Patience	I see. So, according to you, it is okay to be rude because you are tired? Let me ask you, Lily; how are your relationships?

Lily	Some are good; some are not. It all depends!
Patience	All depends on what?
Lily	It all depends on whether I like them or not.
Patience	Are you actually satisfied with that?
Tony	Lily lowered her head. She had to be honest. She owed it to herself to be sincere. She knew very well that some of her relationships were bad, really bad in fact. She recognized that these failing relationships contributed to her pain.
Lily	No, I am not, she said without daring to look at Patience.
Patience	Of course you're not, Lily. What do you expect, my dear? You want people to be nice to you, but it is okay for you to be rude and disrespectful to them. Then you get angry when they treat you the same way. Don't you? It's okay for you to make demands of others, but it isn't okay when someone has expectations of you. Am I right? It is fine for you to raise your voice, but how do you feel when someone raises their voice to you? You are deliriously happy if people agree with you, but if they don't, watch out! You treat your loved ones with indifference, but you want them to take your feelings into consideration at all times.
Lily thought	That's all true. But how does she know?
Patience	Lily, dear, I sense that you long to have good relationships with the people around you, whether they are your friends or not. You want to get along with everyone, don't you? I can tell that you are yearning for peace and joy, but let me tell you, with the way you are choosing to live your life, you will not get very far. You need to know and understand that if you want people to be courteous to you, you have to be courteous to them. That's the way it works! Of course, there will always be some exceptions, but for the most part, in order to receive, you first have to be willing to give the same things you are asking others to give to you. There is no other way unless you meet people who have already found the fountain. You see, those few people will love you unconditionally. But other than that, people will turn their backs on you, Lily. Nobody likes individuals who are rude and nasty. No one feels comfortable with people who are demanding and manipulative. No one likes to be treated rudely and with indifference. Do you?
Lily thought	Okay, okay, I get it! What do you want from me?

Tony	Lily's eyes were filled with tears. She knew she had not been very nice towards other people. She knew she had a chip on her shoulder and expected others to do things her way. She had not been willing to compromise. She was angry and because of unmet expectations, people got on her nerves very easily. Lily didn't like to be that way, but regardless, that was the way she was. That was why she was searching, and, because she was searching for wisdom to help improve her shortcomings, Lily had already won half of the battle.
	Patience was touched when she saw the tears in Lily's eyes. She leaned forward in the rocking chair and opened her arms. Lily sat in her lap and leaned into the welcoming arms that embraced her. Lily pressed so close to Patience that she could hear the beating of her heart.
Patience	It's okay Lily, weep. Weep all you want. It hurts. I know it hurts. Here I am. Let it out. Just let it out.
Tony	Lily cried and cried, holding on to Patience, whose hands were rubbing her back. Lily needed Patience so badly and kept on crying until she fell asleep in those loving arms. She was holding her in such a wonderful caring way. Lily was simply not used to feeling that kind of affection.
	Patience looked at Lily, asleep in her arms, like a child who had just found a safe place to rest. Patience rocked Lily for a while, looking at her with eyes full of love and compassion.
Patience	This is good; this is very good. Tears cleanse the soul. Lily, you are getting closer to the fountain, the source of all things, and your broken heart is in the process of being restored.
Tony	I was a very impatient individual. I was easily annoyed and irritated by people and things. I knew something inside of me had to change. I had to learn that patience is a quality of the heart that can be achieved with practice. I had to remind myself over and over again to relax. I had to recite to myself: 'Tony, be patient.' Amazingly enough, over time, when I began to connect with my inner self, I began to see a change in my attitude. I was becoming a patient person! Without effort! I realized that it is really not worth it to get upset by the little things in life. And if we do, we are turning away from the fountain.

What we do not understand we do not possess.

Johann Wolfgang von Goethe

Tony	It was a bone-chilling morning. Lily scanned the cloudy sky from her window. Even inside her room, she could feel the cold air on her face seeping through the windowpane. A wave of melancholy and sadness overwhelmed her. She kept on thinking about her conversation with Patience. She was disappointed at how long it was taking for her to reach the light at the end of the tunnel.
Lily thought	I sure have a long way to go.
Tony	She whimpered, and tears leaked out.
	She hadn't noticed that she had company. Hope was standing there, smiling at her with a smooth face, free of worry.
Hope	Are you feeling hopeless, Lily? Don't! I am here for you. I will keep you company, and as I told you before, I will hold you when you need me. Lean on me.
Lily	Oh, Hope, I am so glad you're here. I don't know what to do.
Hope	Oh! Lily, it is not that hard. All you have to do is to treat others the way you want to be treated. That is the formula, you know. If you want love, you have to learn to give love. If you want kindness, learn to be kind. If you want to be respected, learn to respect. If you want to be understood, learn to understand. If you want to be heard, learn to speak up. In other words, you have to be willing to give those things that you want to receive. Think about it. How can you expect someone to be kind to you when you are so rude? How can you expect to be understood when you are not willing to understand? How can you expect to be accepted if all you do is demand from others? I'm sorry, Lily. I don't mean to burst your bubble, honey, but give it up. It doesn't work that way!
Tony	It sure doesn't. It is so true that most people, me included, want to receive but aren't willing to give the very things we ask for. Doesn't that sound a bit crazy to you? We want people to be kind to us but we don't want to be kind to them. Am I missing something here? Are we not aware of the joy that it produces to be kind to others? I know for a fact that kindness brings great pleasure and gratification, because kindness is a beautiful feeling that originates in the soul of men. It can

come forth very easily when we are willing to let it out. Kindness brings a perfect balance within us when it is allowed to flow freely.

Lily	I know, Hope, I know. But it is extremely hard, whined Lily.
Hope	How hard it is depends on what you want, Lily. If you want good relationships, you have to be willing to make the first move, and so far, you haven't. There's an expression: 'If you always do what you always did, you will always get what you always got!' The knowledge doesn't do you any good, honey; it's the doing that will make a difference.
Tony	Hope sat on the chair and gently drew Lily to her lap, looking deep into Lily's eyes and searching her soul. Her voice dropped to a whisper.
Hope	You are hiding behind your walls because you don't want to be hurt. You are afraid to open up to people because you mistakenly believe that people have the power to hurt you. They don't. You give that power to them. Think about it. Hope gave Lily an affectionate pat on the shoulder. Cheer up! It is a beautiful day out there, even if it is cold. Go out and enjoy it. Don't allow the cold weather to dictate what you do today. There is beauty everywhere you look, Lily. You can see it if you look for it.
Tony	Lily dried her tears. She was feeling better already. Hope had indeed lifted her spirit.
Lily thought	What a gift to have found Hope, what a dear friend she is...
Tony	She got ready to go out and enjoy the day. She pulled the curtains back and opened the window. The sun was out and the temperature seemed comfortable enough. Still, Lily put on her heavy winter clothes and her snow boots, since she could see that the snow was piled high along the walk.

Lily went downstairs and ran into the hotel attendant. He bent forward to look for something, paying no attention to Lily. Lily felt awkward, knowing she hadn't been very nice to him, and she was not used to apologizing. Suddenly, she heard Hope's words reverberating in her head, 'if you always do what you always did, you will always get what you always got... The knowledge doesn't do you any good, honey. It's the doing that will make a difference.' She also heard Conscience in her mind saying, 'Lily, you owe him an apology.' Yes, I do, she admitted to herself, as she took a deep breath.

	Lily walked to the counter where the attendant looked at her and politely smiled. 'How can I help you?'
Lily	What's your name?
Tony	'Bill,' he answered.
Lily	Bill, I would like to apologize to you for the way I treated you last night. I am sorry I was so rude. I wasn't feeling very well and took my frustration out on you. Would you please forgive me?
Bill	Thank you, miss. I accept your apology.
Tony	Lily noticed that she felt very good about herself.
Lily thought	This was a big step for me.
Lily	Thank you, Bill!
Tony	A genuinely warm smile greeted him as she walked away. She left the hotel and strolled down the streets of Relationship City. The streets were quite crowded with all kinds of people. Some of them greeted her, but most didn't. People seemed to be in a hurry. Was she invisible to them? They didn't take time to be courteous and considerate to her. It was just like she was used to doing.
Lily thought	That's just the way people are, I suppose. We are too busy doing our own thing.
Tony	Patience and Hope said it was up to her to improve her interaction with others. She was willing to try. She wanted to learn more about people and better understand the human race. She continued walking for a while, observing every individual that crossed her path. Most of them appeared very serious, as though they were trapped within, but there were others who cordially greeted her. After a long walk, she was fatigued. She came to a crowded park and decided to rest for a few minutes. For the first time in ages, and from a different perspective of awareness, she began to carefully observe the people around her. She noticed a mother holding her baby in her arms—there was love. Another woman gave food to the homeless—there was compassion. A young man helped an older man cross the street—there was kindness. Two girls played on the swing set—there was friendship. A man enjoying the beautiful day—there was joy.
	'Good morning, miss. May I sit here?' inquired an older gentleman. At first, Lily didn't know what to say. This is an opportunity to try something different—a new way to act toward people. She was keen to give it a chance.

Lily	Yes, please, sit.
Tony	'Thank you! Beautiful day isn't it?' said the gentleman.
Lily	Yes, it is. Allow me to introduce myself. My name is Lily.
Tony	'Please call me Understanding. And what are you doing here?'
Lily	Oh, I am just people watching.
Understanding	I love people, but most of the time I feel sorry for them.
Lily	Why do you feel sorry for them?
Understanding	Well, they don't know how to relate to each other. They don't know how to love or how to give. Most people want to be understood, but they don't want to go out of their way to understand others, he stressed.
Tony	I, too, was one of those. I wanted people to understand me, but I wasn't making any effort to understand them. But one day I was enlightened! To have meaningful relationships and good communication with others, I realized I must first try to understand others, and not expect them to always understand me. This made an incredible difference. Ever since I applied this piece of wisdom, my relationships have improved tremendously.
Lily	Well, couldn't that be because we don't trust each other?
Understanding	And why don't we trust?
Lily	I don't know. I guess when you get hurt you kind of want to stay away. It has been my experience that when I give to people and love them, I am rejected or betrayed.
Understanding	Yes, many feel as you do, Lily. That is the problem. Most people are afraid of being betrayed, hurt or rejected, and so, very few are willing to take a risk.
Lily	Why would I put myself in a situation where I know that I'll be hurt?
Understanding	How can you know that?
Lily	Because...
Understanding	Because why?
Lily	Because that's just the way people are! They hurt others. They use you, and if a person is nice, they take advantage of you.
Understanding	You really feel that way, huh? Is that what you do to others?

Lily	Of course not, but that is simply the way other people are to each other.
Understanding	Oh, Lily, that is not always the case. There are also nice people out there. If you stop and see, you will notice that the majority of people are nice. Look Lily, you feel the way you do because you are expecting something in return if you are nice to a person. You need to detach yourself and not entertain expectations. People can only respond from what they know. It is the same way with you. You can only give what you can at every given moment. If you learn to lower your expectations of others, then you can freely give to them and freely receive from them.
Lily	Tell me how that works.
Understanding	The expectations you have of others are the cause of your pain. They actually put you in bondage. Does that make sense? In other words, if you accept people as they are, you can also accept yourself as you are, which will set you free. However, it's only when you allow others to be free that you can free yourself.
Lily	Could you be more specific, please?
Understanding	People are trapped. Even though they don't trust each other, they depend on one another. They try to possess each other.
Lily	I don't understand that. We all depend on each other for all kinds of things, don't we?
Understanding	I am talking about depending on someone psychologically and emotionally. If you are depending on another human being for your happiness, soon you start demanding that other people contribute to your fulfillment and well-being. You cannot live your life expecting other people to do that for you. They can't! Nor can you live your life doing things for others just so they will like you and accept you.
Tony	This was a very important lesson for me. I had to learn to break free from the heavy chains of codependency. I realized that my fears were a result of that bondage, caused by my belief that someone else was the source of my happiness and self-worth. I had to understand in my heart that my happiness doesn't come from anyone. As a result, I learned not to demand happiness from others. I found myself in a place where I was no longer attached to anyone for a sense of self-esteem. The only thing that you can do for others is to love them—to love them unconditionally.

Lily	Oh, come on! Who can do that? No one can love in such a way, she said, rolling her eyes.
Understanding	No, not on their own, they can't.
Lily	Now what do you mean? Lily was getting impatient.
Understanding	What I mean is that no one is capable of unconditional love, unless, of course, they have found the fountain within.
Tony	That's true, no one is able to love unconditionally without wisdom and knowledge. It is my experience that I could draw real love from the fountain. But before I could, I needed to understand all about the fountain. To me, unconditional love means to accept others the way they are and not taking their behavior personally. This is a difficult lesson to learn. I'm actually still trying to master it. I am learning that it works, at least for me, when I don't judge or try to be possessive of the other person. I find freedom when I accept without expectations what people could offer to me. As a result, I find myself free to give. It is a nice position. All the illusions I had about people and myself are getting weaker and weaker as I continue walking on the path of spiritual growth.

Understanding could see everything. He knew Lily was searching to fill the void of her soul. He could see she wanted to be whole.

Understanding	You seem to be searching for the fountain.
Lily	Yes, I am. I have been traveling a long journey to find it. I have discovered parts of it along the way that are helping me walk toward it, but I have not yet been able to find it entirely. You don't happen to know how to get there, do you?
Understanding	Of course I know! I am a part of it, just like everyone else you have met. The fountain has sent us directly to you. You must embrace us. You must listen to us. We are here to help you find your way. Keep going Lily. You are getting closer and closer. I will be with you. Do you remember what Conscience told you?
Lily	She told me so many things. What exactly are you referring to?
Understanding	She told you she is the voice of the fountain. Do you remember that?
Lily	Yes, I do.

Understanding	Well, I am the eyes of the fountain. I am the one who will help you see. I will help you see beauty. There is splendor and magnificence everywhere, Lily. The fountain is preparing you to see it.
Lily	Oh, Understanding, it has been such a long journey. I am so eager to find the fountain. I am becoming more and more aware as I go along that everything that I need to satisfy the thirst of my soul is in the fountain.
Understanding	Yes, Lily. The fountain is the light of your being. It is the spiritual bread. It is the water that quenches the thirsty soul. You are so close, Lily, so close.
Lily	But, if I am so close, why do I feel this heaviness?
Understanding	Have you thought about forgiveness? Usually, when a person feels a heavy heart, it's because they are carrying a grudge. It may be toward someone else or even toward one's self. Have you considered that?
Lily	Yes, I have, but I haven't been able to escape from the grip of resentment and guilt. She recalled what Forgiveness had said: 'Lily, when you won't forgive from your heart, you really only punish yourself.'
Understanding	You are still hiding behind your walls. You're afraid to come out because you believe people have power to hurt you. They don't! There isn't a person on earth that has the power to make you unhappy or disturb your peace of mind, but because of your current lack of inner vision and understanding you still believe that if you forgive, you will expose yourself to being hurt again. So you have unconsciously decided that it's easier to hold on to your anger and resentment as a shield. But let me tell you, forgiving others will benefit you more than them. Do you really want to live the rest of your life like that?
Tony	Lily began to realize the importance of Forgiveness. It became clear that she needed to forgive others and let's not forget, she needed to ask for forgiveness herself. She had hurt others just as much as they had hurt her. In the quietness of her heart, Lily cried out 'Forgiveness, please come into my heart! Oh, Forgiveness, I need you!'
	Understanding looked at her with an abundance of love and tenderness, then he spoke.
Understanding	When Forgiveness inhabits your heart, you will feel like a new person. I promise!
Lily	But, how do I forgive?

Understanding	The fountain will make it possible for you to choose forgiveness. You forgive when you are no longer providing a home in your mind to unforgiving thoughts.
Lily	Could you be more explicit, please?
Understanding	Lily, when you find the fountain, you are going to be transformed. That is a change that takes place within; a change of heart. This change among other things, allows you to forgive and to understand the purpose of your life.
Lily	...and what is the purpose of my life?
Understanding	Because you have a hunger for spiritual food, the purpose of your life is to find the fountain. When you find it, Lily, you will experience real love—love that supersedes reason and logic.
Lily	Is it the same way for everybody?
Understanding	We are not talking about everybody, Lily. We are talking about you, but, yes! It is the same way for everybody, in the fullness of time!
Lily	Okay, but where is the fountain? Where is wisdom?
Understanding	Wisdom and the fountain are one, Lily.
Lily	But, how will I know if I have found the fountain?
Understanding	You will know. The fountain will reveal itself to you. Wisdom says, 'If you look for me with all your heart, you will find me.' Are you looking for wisdom with all your heart, Lily?
Lily	I believe I am.
Understanding	Then don't worry or dismay. Wisdom will manifest itself to you in the fullness of time.
Lily	What do you mean by 'in the fullness of time?'
Understanding	I mean, when you are truly ready, or in other words, when the time is right. Always remember that wisdom is never early, nor is it ever late. It is always right on time.
Tony	It was getting dark. Lily looked at her watch and realized that it was time to go.
Lily	It is getting late. It was a pleasure talking to you, sir. Thank you for the advice. I will definitely keep it in mind.
Understanding	Don't just keep it in mind, Lily. Apply it in your life and see the difference. Nothing will change unless you choose to change your thinking and behavior. When you are finally so sick of your illusions that you let go of them, the change will

take place. No one changes until that precise moment. You are part of something wonderful that you have not fully grasped. But, you are getting there. Compared to the day you began your journey, you have so much more knowledge, power and understanding. Always remember that, and don't sell yourself short.

Tony

Everyone Lily met along the way had been expressing things she already knew in some deep corner of her heart, but had not yet accessed. However, she was getting very close to the fountain. When she gets there, all the pieces of the puzzle of her life will fall into place.

Chapter Five: Religion City

There is wisdom in youth and there is wisdom in age.
One is loud and seeking, the other one is silent and true.

Chief Dan George

Tony

Lily spent some time going back and forth from one city to the next, trying to increase her knowledge and understanding. She was attempting to apply the lessons she had learned. Many times she was successful, and many times she wasn't. Her newly acquired awareness helped her make better choices. Her relationships with people improved, and the expectations she had of others and of herself lessened. Nevertheless, she had not yet made the connection with the fountain, and therefore, the pain of her heart was not yet relieved, nor the thirst of her soul satisfied. Lily was trying too hard to understand logically the things of the Spirit. She was using logic and reasoning to try to make sense of everything that happened to her. She was analyzing every single thing to death. The truth was that Lily had not yet recognized that in order to reach the fountain, she needed to rely on the Spirit to guide her, teach her, and comfort her.

> I can understand, Lily. I went back and forth in my mind trying to make sense of everything myself. I believed that if I could understand with reason and logic the things of the Spirit, I would be able to reach the fountain. Wrong! I was dead wrong! The matters of the Spirit can only be understood in the Spirit. Reasoning and logic are thick walls standing in the way of the spiritual realm. I didn't believe it before, but based on what I have learned and experienced, I can tell that only those who are able to go beyond reason and logic are able to make the connection, feel the indwelling presence of the fountain, and experience a joy that cannot be fathomed by the mind.

'Come higher, Lily,' a soft and sweet voice whispered to the deepest part of her soul. Lily stopped to listen. 'Come higher, Lily. I am waiting for you.' Lily didn't know what to think.

Lily thought   Surely, it's only my imagination.

Tony	She went to the station to catch the next train. The train was not scheduled to leave until late that evening, so she had approximately five hours to wait. She sat down in the waiting area, picked up a magazine, and attempted to read. Lily greeted a young woman who sat next to her and then continued reading.
	The woman turned to her and said, 'You have had a pain in your heart for a long time.
	Lily raised her eyebrows in surprise.
Lily thought	How does she know that?
Tony	She was baffled. Lily was so startled she looked at the woman unable to speak.
	So the young woman repeated, 'You have had a pain in your heart since you were fifteen years old.'
Lily thought	I heard you the first time! How does she know that? That's what I want to know!
Tony	The woman appeared to be about twenty-five, but somehow seemed older—not in her physique but her maturity. Her eyes revealed that this young woman was a mature soul.
	'My name is Deborah. What's yours?'
Lily	It's Lily, she answered coldly, not engaging in any other pleasantries.
Lily thought	If you know about my pain, shouldn't you know my name?
Deborah	Do you know why you have that pain in your soul?
Tony	Lily was taken off guard. She did not know how to reply to such a question, and responded inside by raising her emotional walls, like she always did when confronted. She looked at Deborah without saying a word.
Deborah	You have pain in your heart because you need prayer in your life.
Lily	I don't need prayer in my life, she snapped.
Deborah	Oh, but you do, Lily …
Tony	Lily's greatest problem was that she no longer believed in answered prayer. She had prayed many times in the past, but according to her, the prayers were never answered. So, eventually Lily became angry at God, furious even. As far as she was concerned, God had failed her. Before she launched

her journey, Lily had reached out to God for healing of her broken heart, but God had not come to her rescue, or so she thought. Lily was devastated. God didn't care. The faith she had as a child had been blown away. It was nowhere to be found. It was gone, gone, gone! Lily found herself facing the trials of each day all by herself. She had no place to find refuge or comfort and hence, the pain of her broken heart got worse. Lily wanted to control her circumstances and believed that the fountain would be found once she learned to unleash her own power.

Even at this point in her journey, Lily just didn't understand God.

> Neither did, I, once upon a time. Lily didn't know, nor could she see, that God was already coming to her rescue. The problem was that Lily expected to even control God. I did too. I was making requests of God, using him to get what I wanted. I ended up very disappointed since I was expecting God to use his magic wand to do whatever I asked. Well, I learned the hard way. I learned that God doesn't work that way and I see now that I would never get anywhere with such an attitude. I began to learn and understand who God really is, or at least, who He really is, for me. What a difference it made in my heart when I discovered the truth! That discovery is the truth that God dwells in me, that God and I are One, and he alone can meet my every need. God is the source from where I can learn the wisdom needed to live one day at a time. Lily will come to that place too. Eventually, it will be made known to her that her heart aches because she is missing the presence—the essence—of God in her heart. That's what happened to me. That's how I know.

Lily   Pardon me! she angrily spat back at Deborah, and then sarcastically asked: Are you going to talk to me about God and Jesus Christ?

Deborah   I would like to.

Lily   Thanks, but I am not interested whatsoever. I don't believe in either one anymore.

Tony   Lily stood, gathered up her belongings, and started to walk away. Deborah took Lily's arm and held on for a moment. She looked straight into Lily's eyes.

Deborah   You and I are going to meet again, Lily, because God wants to heal you.

Lily thought	Yeah, right; whatever. Just let me out of here, was the response building up in Lily.
Lily	Please leave me alone!
Deborah	I cannot leave a soul in pain, answered Deborah with a serious countenance. I can help you, Lily. Please let me help you.
Lily	I don't need your help, said Lily, and arrogantly walked away.
Tony	A couple of years ago, Keith and I took a trip to the Grand Canyon. One day when we were contemplating this amazing creation, he got very thoughtful; he was deep in thought. He turned and looked at me with a serious gaze.
Keith	Tony, where do men without God find healing for their pain and sorrow? Where are broken hearts restored from the heavy burdens of daily trials and afflictions? How can people reach out to God when they don't even know who God really is? With the newest technology, great advances have been made in almost every area of our lives—but have we come to know God? Have we come to that place of total surrender where we can rest in the knowledge and understanding of God's presence deep within the depths of our beings? Tony, we may have all the things the world has to offer, but without knowledge—the consciousness—of God's spirit abiding within us, we have nothing. We are empty and lost with no place to go when we don't have the realization that God's spirit is in us, and it is precisely the Spirit of God within us that will guide our every step and set us free from fear.
Tony	Lily wandered aimlessly around the train station, trying to put Deborah out of her mind. No matter where she walked, she could not forget the encounter. A nagging feeling told her to listen to Deborah.
Lily thought	No way! This is just too weird.
Tony	The train finally pulled into the station. Lily boarded and kept her eyes peeled for Deborah, who was nowhere around.
Lily thought	Good, that's a relief.
Tony	The train was almost full. Lily eventually found a seat near the rear of the car. She sat and continued thinking about Deborah. She just couldn't get over the experience.

Lily thought	Who was this woman? How did she know about my pain? This kind of thing doesn't happen in the real world. What is the meaning of it?
Tony	It was dark outside. All Lily could see were the lights shining through the windows of the homes along the way. Eventually she dozed off.
	'Ladies and gentlemen,' announced the train conductor, 'Welcome to Religion City.' Lily could not believe her ears. Surely she had made a mistake! She didn't want to go to Religion City.
Lily	Excuse me, she said to the conductor. My destination is the City of the Spirit.
Tony	'Oh, then miss, you took the wrong train.'
Lily	That's impossible.
Tony	'Well, miss, we're in Religion City.'
Lily	When does the train depart for the City of the Spirit?
Tony	'I don't know. There was a severe blizzard and the roads are blocked with massive snow drifts. It's possible that we won't be able to get out of here for a week.'
Lily	You said a week? You can't be serious! I don't even want to be here for an hour. I definitely don't want to be stuck here a week.
	'I'm sorry, miss. There is nothing I can do about bad weather. You will have to wait like everyone else.'
Lily thought	Oh, no! What am I going to do? This is the one place I don't want to be.
Tony	Lily had had very bad experiences with religion in the past. It had instilled dread and fear in her. God had been portrayed as someone mean, standing with a whip, ready to beat her if she did not behave as the church said she should. Lily felt fear and anxiety over the concept of God portrayed by the religious people in her life. She wanted no part of it.
	Lily left the station with a heavy heart. For some reason, the pain deep in her soul grew until it was almost unbearable. She walked toward the center of town, looking for a place to stay. After a while, she found a bed & breakfast, where she decided to stay. She left her luggage and went to the laundromat. Lily read a book while she waited for her clothes to finish washing. Someone walked into the laundromat. Lily

looked up to see who had entered. She gasped: Deborah! Lily wanted to hide.

Deborah noticed Lily out of the corner of her eye, but ignored her. Lily froze. But after a few minutes, Lily decided to approach her.

Lily	You said you could help me. How can you help me?
Deborah	I can help you by praying for you.
Lily	What good would that do if I don't pray for myself?
Deborah	I will pray that all the obstacles in your path be removed.
Lily	Is that it? She asked rolling her eyes.
Deborah	No, I will also counsel you and help you understand who God really is.
Lily	Hmm... I'm not sure... Thanks anyway, and she started to walk back to her chair.
Deborah	Before you go, here's my phone number and address in case you change your mind.
Lily	Thank you.
Tony	Afterwards Lily and Deborah went their separate ways.

Religion City was a very large city. There were so many churches everywhere that it was overwhelming.

Lily thought If religion is so good for you, how come there are so many different denominations?

Tony Lily's heart needed spiritual food so badly that she decided to give Religion City another try. She stepped into one of the churches and asked to speak with the pastor. She was invited to wait for Barney, a counselor in the matters of the soul for seventeen years. Barney led Lily to his office. He showed all smiles, at first. Lily sat across from him and began asking him questions—questions Barney could not answer, and he didn't like it. Barney, who labeled himself as a human representative of God here on earth, was such a self-righteous man. He was full of pride and arrogance. When Barney couldn't answer Lily's questions, he became defensive and rude, even unloving towards Lily. He felt Lily was challenging him, but she really wasn't. She was only asking him what was troubling her heart. Barney fell short with his answers, and his behavior left a lot to be desired. He became very nasty and dismissed Lily in an offensive manner.

Lily thought	I just wanted to punch him in the nose. If this is what it means to be a Christian, thank you very much, but no thank you.
Tony	She was crying as she left.
	God is a banquet, but counselors like Barney starve people to death.
Lily thought	Isn't he supposed to be a loving pastor? Don't they preach that God is love?
Tony	Lily tried finding the answers through the Churches in Religion City. Jesus is the Lord and Savior of the world, they preached. Lily did not believe in the principles of the Church, at least the way they presented them. She met many people who claimed to have Jesus in their lives, but they often still seemed empty. She had heard many people say that Jesus is love, but she didn't see much evidence of that love in their lives. She had seen plenty of people at these churches lifting their hands in praise to God, in the name of Jesus, yet when they left the church their hearts were bitter and judgmental.
Lily thought	I just don't believe in religion! I am sure religion works for some, and I respect their point of view, but for me, there must be another way to find God. I will not find God here, I'm sure of that, and I just don't want to be here anyway... it doesn't feed my soul, on the contrary, it instills fear in me.
Tony	Lily's pain was no longer bearable. She didn't know what to do. She had tried every avenue available to her but all to no avail. She put her hands in her pockets, trying to keep them warm from the chilly weather. Tears were running down her face. There was a folded piece of paper in her left pocket. What's this? Lily took it out and saw it was Deborah's number and address.
	She took the city bus to see Deborah.
Lily thought	Maybe she will have some answers. Maybe she can help me. Let me hear more of what she has to say.
Tony	Lily knocked on the door. She didn't notice that Deborah was right there sitting on the enclosed front porch, writing in what looked like a journal. Deborah opened the screen door. Lily felt quite awkward and didn't quite know what to say...
Lily	Here I am. You may talk to me, but I warn you, I am not going to believe just because of what you say. If it is true that

	God talks to you, he will have to show himself to me too. I am no different than you.
Deborah	He wants to talk to you, Lily.
Lily	We'll see. Because so far, he hasn't!
Tony	Deborah requested that Lily sit down, so she made herself comfortable on the sofa. She felt the pressure of her past issues with religion building up inside—making her feel as though her chest would explode. The mere thought of being there caused a nervous shiver from head to toe.
	Deborah offered her a cup of hot tea. Then she sat next to Lily.
Deborah	Listen to me, Lily. I am going to tell you something that I'd like you to ponder. I will make no attempt whatsoever to force you to believe. What I am going to do is share with you what I know, what I've experienced. If you profit from it, fine; if you don't, well...
	Always remember that God is not some mystical being out there somewhere. He is inside of you.
Tony	Deborah took Lily's hand in hers and there was gentleness in her voice.
Deborah	Do you understand what I am telling you, dear? God is the provider of all things. Before you can experience a difference in your life, you first have to learn to trust God with all your heart and learn to love him with all your mind and soul. God knows your heart and even your thoughts. He loves you just the way you are. You have to learn to thank Him for the good and the bad that you have been through.
Tony	I choose to believe that God, the Creator, is Perfect Love. Therefore, God cannot see faults in me nor in you. How could Perfect Love see error? This thought has helped me get rid of a lot of guilt and fear towards God.
	Lily shook her head in disbelief. Her morale plummeted. She felt as if she had been punched in her stomach. Deborah's statement made Lily irate. Each word resonated like a stone hitting the bottom of a cliff.
Lily	That's too hard! I don't believe I can love and trust God with all my heart and soul. How can anyone do that? I already tried trusting Him and He let me down. How can someone thank him for the bad things?
Lily thought	I won't be able to do that. I just can't. It's impossible!

Lily	How can I love and trust God, Deborah? How? How can I love and trust a God that is deaf to a person's needs? Lily's whole demeanor displayed anger.
Deborah	Why are you so angry? Why do you feel that way?
Lily	Why? Because on many occasions, I have tried to reach out to God, and I have never heard him talk to me or answer any of my prayers. That's why!
Deborah	God will speak to you, Lily. You must be patient, and you must be still and listen.
Lily thought	Oh, yeah, that's what you all say. He will speak to you... He will answer your prayers, but he never does.
Deborah	You have the wrong idea about God, Lily. You haven't experienced who God really is.
Lily	Excuse me! What do you mean I don't know God? I have been preached to about him all my life, so please don't YOU tell me that I don't know him.
Tony	Now she was livid.
Deborah	You don't know him, Lily. You have just heard about him, but you don't know his heart. I will introduce you to him, Lily. I will hold your hand and bring you to the one who will make the heart of the Father known to you.
Lily	How are you going to do that? A glimmer of hope spread over Lily's face.
Tony	Deborah just smiled tenderly, as if she knew something that would make all the difference.
Deborah	You will have to trust me on that one. If I tell you right now you wouldn't understand. I don't want to risk you running away from God again. Just trust me, Lily. Come visit me again and we'll talk. I can help you understand. Before you can fully trust God, you must get yourself on solid ground. Your heart needs to be uplifted and your anger dispelled.
Tony	The room grew quiet as Deborah stood there a minute, letting everything sink in.
Deborah	God has brought you to me, Lily. As I said to you before, God wants to heal your broken heart. Don't ignore his call. He wants to fill you with the love you hunger for. Answer God's invitation. Come unto him with all your heart and soul. Give to him your past, present, and future. Turn over to him the bare and empty life you have been living. Then you will find true freedom, true happiness, true peace and true love, and

	as a result, you will have hope for the future. Lily's head was spinning and she felt light-headed. She fanned her face, trying to get a little air. Sweat was dripping down the middle of her back.
Lily	I just don't believe it, Deborah, I really wish I did, but I don't.
Deborah	Maybe, just maybe, you are afraid to believe.
Lily	I don't believe God the way he is portrayed by the church. Sorry, but I don't.
Lily thought	What do you want me to do? Do you want me to force myself to believe in him? I don't think so. Either I believe, or I don't.
Deborah	Neither do I. God is so much more. He is the fountain inside you. Lily, when you understand this, you will realize that that's the only purpose worthy enough for us human beings—to express that love. Only God's love, not emotional love, fulfills us completely. Without God's love in your heart, you have nothing. Absolutely nothing!

**If you do not change direction,
you may end up where you are headed.**

Lao Tzu

Tony	Lily decided to stay longer in Religion City and visit regularly with Deborah, who was providing much needed answers. During one of their visits, Deborah had invited another friend, an older man named Jack. Deborah thought Jack could reach out to Lily better than she could. They spent several hours talking about God. Lily was impressed with Jack. Outwardly, Jack wore modest clothing, but within, he wore love and kindness. Lily observed Jack for a while. She couldn't take her eyes off him. He was a sweet old man. His blue eyes were pools reflecting a peaceful soul. When Jack spoke to her, he made her feel so loved and understood, and showed patience towards her. There was positively no judgment.
Lily thought	I want what he has.
Jack	Listen carefully to me now, Lily. God is a God of great love. The wall inside you, blocking the flow of his love, will be removed. Once you glimpse the ever-present light, you will start throwing away all those beliefs that hide the existence of God from you.

Lily	How do I start?
Jack	You start when you face your misconceptions about God. You have to get rid of the misunderstandings that religious people have fed you.
Lily	I suspect I have a lot of those.
Jack	It is very hard to find God in religion because religion is external. Religion is a series of rituals and dogmas made by men. They have little to do with the true essence of God. The danger of religion is that the blessed sacraments become more important than God. Keeping the Sabbath becomes more important than human beings. Spirituality, on the other hand, is to be aware of what you're saying, thinking, doing, acting, and being aware that God's children do not live their lives based on the law of men. God's children live their lives based on the law of God.
Lily	What is the law of God?
Jack	Love, Lily. The law of God is love. That's it! God's will is that we love him, and that we love one another and ourselves. Love is something that originates within. God is love and his love will enter your heart, if you will allow it. All you have to do is say, 'I want this. I want to see and experience God's love.'
Tony	A scoff spread on Lily's face.
Lily	Come on, Jack, if it was that simple, everyone would be experiencing God's love, but they're not.
Jack	People have to open themselves to receive his love.
Lily	I have tried to open myself to receive God's love, protested Lily, but I haven't been able.
Jack	Stop trying. You cannot do it, so give it up.
Lily	But you just said that people have to open themselves to receive his love. You lost me, Jack.
Jack	You see, when you give up, when you surrender your life to love, you become open to receive. Pure and real love is not something you can produce, Lily. This kind of love is imparted in you by the presence of God in your heart.
	Let me add something else. The day will come when you will understand that God and love are one. You will also comprehend the meaning of unconditional love. Lily, only God can love you in such a way. Listen to me. I have walked in your shoes. Don't close your heart, Lily. When you begin

to glimpse the truth that God loves you just the way you are, you'll begin to enter into the rest that is found in the arms of love. Climb higher, Lily. Do not be afraid to reach out to God. I guarantee you that if you reach out to him, you will not be disappointed.

Lily

But hold on, Jack, I tried reaching out to God and was disappointed because he didn't reach out to me. It was very painful—a pain I really don't want to go through again. It hurt too much, and I'm afraid my heart would not recover if I am rejected again this time.

Jack

Lily, just like heaven is above the earth, God's ways are above our ways. The basic principle of God's dealings with man is not to be found in human reasoning and understanding, but by the revelation of God's Spirit. As we draw near to God, we find that he draws near to us. I believe that it is God's will, that each of us might know him—that we might know his true nature. There is a continual seeking going on in the depths of your heart for God, and I can assure you that to a sincere call of the heart, the Spirit of God responds. The more we seek to know him in the understanding of our own minds, the less we find he responds; but, if in childlike simplicity we turn over control to him, we find a response directly from the heart of God.

Come here, Lily; Let me hold you. Lily moved to the edge of the chair, and Jack embraced her with so much compassion. She felt his loving arms around her. Can you feel the love in my heart for you?

Lily

Oh, yes, I do. It feels wonderful.

Jack

It is God loving you through me and hugging you through my arms. God reveals himself to us in so many ways, Lily. Sometimes, he chooses to manifest his presence in a mystical way, like your encounter with Deborah. Other times, he chooses to manifest himself through the beauty of his creation, like gorgeous scenery that no one could have created but God. He touches our hearts through the sound of music or through magnificent pieces of art. But mostly, God wants to reveal his presence—his essence—through us. That's why it is so important that we open our hearts to him. He's always ready and willing to fill us with unconditional love for others and for ourselves. As human beings, we can't love in that special way, Lily. Only God can, and he uses us to let his love flow. I don't question whether God is real; I just accept that he is. I just receive his love without questioning it. Can you reach for that place inside you, Lily?

Tony	Lily closed her eyes. A sense of comfort and security swept over her. She wasn't sure what was going on, but somehow, she felt protected, cared about, and understood.
Lily	Jack, please share more of God with me, pleaded Lily, wiping some tears.
Jack	God is the Spirit who lives within you. He is your Creator. He is the one knocking at the door of your heart, asking you to open so that he may fill you with his presence, which is love itself.
Lily	Okay, Jack, I hear you. But, if everyone could open the door of their hearts to God, wouldn't they? Who wants to live in darkness? No one! So you're saying that we just don't know how to open the door because we have been taught so many different things about him. I don't think it is fair for God to expect us to open the door to him when we don't really know him. How can I open the door to God if all I hear is that God will punish me if I don't? Who wants a God like that? I don't believe that I should come to God out of fear. Do you?
Jack	No. No, I don't. I believe that we can only come to God when we acknowledge his existence—and when we come to him, open-hearted, willing to shed the baggage that we've been harboring in the deepest, darkest part of our souls. God already knows what you need to let go of, but he wants you to fundamentally acknowledge it to yourself as well, and see exactly what's been stored away as your own thoughts and beliefs. When we acknowledge these false beliefs, healing takes place, and we begin seeing God as our friend. He is a personal God, and when we see him as a friend, we have a spiritual life and we can have it in abundance.
Lily	Spiritual abundance is a new concept. What does it mean?
Jack	It means there is never too much of God. It also means you can rest in God. God is not an empty philosophy—not a dogma, a creed, nor some empty concept—but a vital, living, omnipresence. God is the center of everyone's love and the source of everyone's hope.
Lily	But that is not what I see in everyone.
Jack	I certainly agree with you. People don't know God. He has so much to give, but people are blind. The law of men is controlling them. They don't have a personal relationship with God. It's the personal relationship that makes the difference.

Lily	What do you mean when you say the law of men is controlling them?
Jack	I mean that many people are more concerned with the dogmas and rituals of the church than they are with having a personal relationship with God. Multitudes are following the doctrine instead of following the Spirit. Many more are abiding in the man-made church instead of abiding in God, the real Church.
Lily	How can I have a personal relationship?
Jack	Well, you invite him to live in your heart and mind.
Lily	I have met people who have invited him to live in their hearts, and I don't see the spiritual abundance you are talking about. I don't see them resting in God.
Jack	I know, and it breaks my heart. People don't have abundant life because they're not willing to let God take control of their lives. It is only when people allow the will of God to guide their lives that they are able to rest. There are many people who have come to God simply because they are terrified to go to hell for eternity. There are others who have come to God because they believe if they come to him, everything will be okay—everything will work out the way they want it. Most people look for God only when they need something. Only a few are willing to follow his lead.
Tony	Lily stared at Jack. Jack certainly spoke with knowledge and understanding.

Jack seemed to have grasped the meaning of God. I can tell by the love and kindness that abide in his spirit.

Lily pinpointed what made Jack different. Jack had the nature of God in his heart. His life showed so much loving kindness and understanding in his disposition.

Lily thought	This is exactly what I am searching for.
Tony	Now she was open to listening to the wisdom Jack had acquired in his own journey. She was willing to accept Jack's teachings because he had what she desired in her own life. He was the wisest man she had ever met. She welcomed what Jack had to say and she felt free to ask him all her questions. Jack never, ever scolded her or judged her—never! What a loving man was Jack. He became Lily's mentor, and by his own example, he taught Lily the way to the heart of God.

I am very fortunate to have discovered that to dwell in God is to find security and rest for which my longing soul has earnestly prayed. I was able to see, with inner eyes, that in this world I have no secure dwelling place, but I have one in God's realm. God is love. He who dwells in love dwells in God and God in him. It was very hard for me to understand God's love, because the love of God literally surpasses human understanding. The Spirit must reveal it to us. But today, after my own long journey, I can feel like I'm totally immersed in God's love and know that the waters supporting me are the waters of his love and kindness. I know that he is the love within me and I find peace as I rest in his presence. Deep in my heart, I pray that someday everyone will feel like Jack does, abiding with God constantly, safe within him every moment.

Fear God, yes, but don't be afraid of Him.

J.A. Spender

Jack   Lily, you need God badly. But your misconceptions are holding you back.

Lily   Well, that's because—no disrespect intended to you—I don't get the same loving attitude you display, from some of the other people I've met who claim to have God in their lives. No offense to anyone, but that's how I feel!

Jack   I know exactly what you mean. I have gone through that too. But Lily, you cannot allow other people to be a stumbling block or stop you from knowing the very essence of God. Don't allow some people's shortcomings and ignorance of God to rob you of your own blessings. They don't mean any harm. Just like you, they are doing the best they can. Everyone is carrying a burden, Lily.

Lily   I'm listening, Jack, but I must make a confession to you. I would be ashamed if others thought of me the way I think about some religious people.

Jack   Would you tell me how you feel about them?

Lily   Well, you know, preaching but not converting, and judging others without looking at their own imperfections.

Jack   I appreciate how you feel, but you have no control over how other people act. As I said before, you cannot allow them to interfere with your path to God. This is your life, Lily, and only you can choose to know God. You have to be willing to seek the answers for yourself and stop judging God based on the shortcomings of others. What you do is for you and not for anyone else.

Tony

This was a hard pill to swallow. Just like Lily, I felt disenchanted by some so-called religious people. However, I had to understand my mistake in condemning them just because they didn't live up to my expectations. Since each person's spiritual journey is traveled at a different speed, it was ignorant of me to measure others with my own yardstick. But now I know that I cannot judge what God is doing in them. I don't know how much light and truth has fallen on their pathway.

Lily

I have another concern. Based on what I have seen and heard, following God can be really devastating. God might want to send me as missionary to Africa. I just wouldn't want to do that, Jack. Or I might be asked to go knocking on neighbors' doors to preach the Gospel. It appears very hard. And come on, Jack, everything seems to be a sin! According to those who claim to know the way, following God means to stop enjoying the pleasures of life. I would have to stop living! Otherwise, they say I will be doomed, and God will remove my name from his list.

Jack

Oh no, my dear, life never gives you anything that you cannot handle, Lily. Missionary people are not distressed doing God's work. On the contrary, they enjoy doing it. This is their calling. That's why they can do it with love and servants' hearts. It is an honor to be in service to God. If God wants you to be a missionary, you'll hear the calling and know the desire to be one. If you don't, it means your calling is to do something else. It's that simple! God doesn't want you to preach the Gospel. *He wants you to live it!*

Lily

That's exactly what I mean, Jack! I don't think I can live the perfect life described in the Gospel. There is no way.

Tony

Lily was troubled.

Lily

I make too many mistakes and have too many spiritual shortcomings.

Jack

All God wants from you, Lily, is that you love him. That's it! When you love God, love him with all your heart, soul, and mind. Love is the very nature of God's spirit. If everything you do is done with love, you will be doing God's will. It's that plain and simple.

Now, let's consider your second concern Lily. Because you don't know God personally yet, you cannot comprehend that it is precisely when God lives in the heart of a believer, that they begin to know abundant life. You don't stop enjoying life, but rather you find a balance and the wisdom to discern.

Lily

What are you trying to tell me?

Jack

There are some pleasures that will harm you, Lily, if they have the upper hand in your life and control your will. When you come to God, your mind is made anew. God's presence within you gives you the strength—the awareness—to overcome any controlling force. God wants you to enjoy life. He wants you to be under his guidance and have balance in your life. You don't want to be overpowered by the weakness of your flesh, do you, Lily?

Tony

Lily was engrossed!

Lily

Well, Jack, I hear what you are saying, and it sounds really good, but I still don't really believe that God will do anything for me. I believe I have to do it myself. And I doubt that God, in a blink of an eye, will remove my pain. I wish I believed, but I don't. What more can I tell you?

Jack

There isn't anything that God cannot do. Nothing is impossible for him. God can heal every heart and enter every life that will receive him, Lily. The hope of the lost soul rests in God. It does not rest in dogmas or in mental comprehension. It rests in the revelation of the Holy Spirit, who lives in every heart but it only manifests to the hearts of those who desire it.

When you invite God to come into your heart, the Spirit of God will manifest in you. The Spirit of God will guide you, teach you, and comfort you. Where the Spirit of God is, there is freedom; there is liberty, complete liberation from every earthly chain, and the bondage you have created for yourself. But this freedom, this liberation, rests in the personal knowledge of who God really is in you, and who you are in him.

Lily

What do I have to do to really know God?

Jack

You must open your heart to the mind of God already inside you. Then you will become aware of the Holy Spirit at work within you. Walk with God. Let him show you the way. Invite him into your heart, and you will experience the indwelling presence of the fountain.

Lily

Why do I have to invite him? If God is all powerful, why doesn't he just come on in?

Jack   Because you have to exercise your free will and choose to let him in. Then you will be open to hear his voice and the personal relationship begins.

Dare to be wise; begin!
He who postpones the hour of living rightly is like the rustic
who waits for the river to run out before he crosses.

Horace

Tony   Lily was alone now. Jack was gone for the day. They had talked for a long time, and Lily had revealed many private thoughts. Jack had shared with her so many things about God, especially God's love. Lily felt different. She felt lighter. Her heart yearned for God's love, and she longed to see God—to see him with the eyes of her heart.

The day was sunny and the temperature was rising. Lily noticed a robin perched on the electrical wires to keep warm. Its chirp was announcing the arrival of spring. Springtime had returned again, and every corner of the countryside had suddenly burst forth with loveliness. Fruit trees and flowers bloomed profusely. Gardens were alive with the new splendor. Lily felt compelled to take a long stroll and meditate on Jack's teachings. She had to admit that she felt at ease with the way Jack spoke about God.

Lily thought   Jack said that wisdom is in God because God is the source of knowledge and understanding. He said that love, peace, hope, patience, forgiveness, and self-control are all part of the fountain. That means, that God *is* Love. God *is* Peace. God *is* Hope. God *is* Patience. God *is* Forgiveness, and Self-Control can be found through the strength of God's power. Oh God, I hope one day I am able to see you the way Jack does.

Tony   She exhaled a sigh of longing.

When I pause to think about it, or about Lily's journey it seems that through Jack, God was reaching out to Lily and touching her soul.

Lily felt the desire to know God on a personal level. She felt a need to experience God in her own life.

I can share with you that to believe in God is good, but to actually experience him, is far better. There is a big difference between doctrine and personal experience.

The days of bondage will soon be over for Lily. Once she invited God into her heart, she will begin the most beautiful relationship she could ever know. She will get to know him as a friend, and walk and talk to him openly. God would impart real faith in her. Once she gets to know him, she will be able to love him. She will be able to trust him, and as a result, she will be able to choose to come out of her bondage into the liberty found in the heart of God, that dwelled in her own being. Lily was on her way to discovering that God is the one who opens the door which leads to the unlimited resources of grace, glory and power. He is the one who makes it possible to share his love and enjoy the richness of his kingdom, right here and now, but we must not forget that this journey to the kingdom of heaven is a process, not a race.

After a long walk through the city streets, Lily met Jack for dinner. She was so happy to see him again, and was bursting with questions. Jack was waiting for her at a table. He smiled a loving smile and looked at her with such kindness.

Lily thought	Thank goodness for Jack!
Jack	Good evening, Lily. It is so nice to see you.
Lily	Oh, Jack, the pleasure is all mine. I went for a long walk and stopped at the station. The train to the City of the Spirit departs tomorrow. I wish you could come with me.
Jack	I will go with you, Lily.
Tony	Jack's reply was evidence that he'd been thinking about Lily's journey too. Lily's heart leapt with Joy.
Lily	You will? She was afraid she might have heard him wrong.
Jack	Yes, I will.
Lily	That's amazing. Why would you go out of your way for me?
Jack	Because I am here to help you find the way. I have been chosen to bring you to the heart of the Father. God is speaking to you through me. I am only a vessel. You must know that it brings me great joy to be the one to hold your hand and take you to the place where you belong.
Lily	Where do I belong, Jack?
Jack	Lily, we all belong in the loving arms of God—the inner fountain.

Lily   Oh Jack, I hunger so much for God's touch. I yearn for God's love and peace so badly that it hurts.

Chapter Six: The City of the Spirit

When you love you should not say, God is in my heart,
but rather, I am in the heart of God.

Kahlil Gibran

Tony	It was morning. The train station was open and people were everywhere. Lily stopped to look at those lost souls with no direction. They reminded her of her own journey. She thought about the day when she arrived at the train station, not knowing where to go. But now, it was different. Lily knew where she was going.
	She was going to the dwelling place of God.
	This time Lily noticed the people in the train. She couldn't believe her eyes: Paul and Rita were on the train.
	Do you remember them? They were the ones she clashed with on her way to Relationship City. They ignored her and she judged them. She had found them rude and nasty!
	Lily could see how wrong she had been about Paul and Rita. They clearly were thirsty for God's love, just like her. She smiled at them. They smiled back! Lily felt compelled to speak to them since she no longer felt angry toward people. On the contrary, she realized that people need each other, so that they may learn from one another. She approached them, followed by Jack, and readily introduced herself. They were very nice and invited her and Jack to sit down and talk.
	'Where are you going?' The couple asked in unison.
Lily	I am going to the City of The Spirit. That's where God lives and I'm going there to meet him, she said with childlike anticipation.
Tony	Paul and Rita smiled and took turns speaking.
Paul	So are we! We are not only going; we are moving to the City of Spirit.
Rita	We have come to realize that if we wish to experience the fullness of God, we need to move to where he lives. At first,

	we didn't want to move, we used to live in Flesh City. While we lived there, we struggled to find happiness.
Paul	But, let me tell you, even though we found great pleasures in Flesh City, we were not complete. For us, Flesh City didn't bring joy. It brought happiness sometimes, but we learned that happiness is something we can have today and lose tomorrow. Joy stays with us regardless. Now we know that joy comes from the awareness of God living within. Have you experienced the presence of God in your heart, Lily?
Lily	No, not yet, she answered, looking at Jack seated peacefully next to her, listening to the conversation.
Paul	What is holding you back?
Tony	Paul's question was straightforward.
Lily	Well, I guess I have too many questions. I am in search of answers that will make sense to me. Unless I understand God, I don't think I will be able to have a personal relationship with him. Maybe I'm wrong.
Paul	I feel the same way as you. If God is not real to me, count me out. The experience of knowing God might work differently for others, but I need this. I need to believe with conviction.
Lily	Thank you, Paul. Just like you, I need to believe with conviction. I don't care to be preached at, nor do I want anyone trying to convert me.
Jack	I totally agree with both of you. But it's been my experience that there are certain things you can never comprehend. There are mysteries that can never be revealed unless you have the realization that the Spirit of God is in your heart. It reveals the truth to you as you go on your journey, one step at a time. People are free to believe whatever they choose; that's their right. We who experience, instead of believe in God, are not here to convert anyone.
Lily	Not convert anyone? Well, that's a surprise!
Jack	No, we are here to share with you the joy, peace, and freedom that we know because of God. We are here to show you based on the way that we respond to the circumstances in our lives—when the heavy storms hit our shores—the serenity and understanding that we find in his presence. We are here to be witnesses, to show you by example, so that you may see him in us and hopefully as a result, want him in your life. That's all. There's no hidden agenda.

Lily	That is exactly why I am listening to you, Jack. I see the Holy Spirit in you. The way you live your life is a testimony that you are truly experiencing God. You are kind, loving and understanding. When I look at you Jack, I can only imagine that if you, as a human, can show such love and wisdom, God must be awesome.
Jack	He is indeed.
Tony	Jack's agreement was heartfelt.
Rita	How can I tell if God lives in my heart?
Jack	You can tell by the fruits of the Spirit.
Lily	What are the fruits of the Spirit?
Jack	Love, joy, peace, forgiveness, understanding, self-control, among others.
Paul	You seem to know a lot about God.
Jack	Oh, no, I don't know a lot *about* God. *I know God!* There is a vast difference, clarified Jack. It is a wonderful thing to know about him, but it is far sweeter to know him. God has touched my soul, and when God does that, we just find within a burning desire to be with him, to be united with him, the source of our origin.
Tony	Lily was reflecting on what Jack just said. She had the desire to return to God. She was hungry to hear more about God. She had an overwhelming need to know him on a personal level.
	Tony, with misty eyes and a jubilant smile, told the audience, God had penetrated Lily's heart with the desire to learn more about him. Lily could no longer run away. God had touched her soul!
	Rita was sitting across from Lily and Jack. She recognized the hunger in Lily's heart. She could see it because she had been there. She had felt the hunger and need to be fed. She knew! Rita had been walking hand in hand with God for a while.
Rita	Do you want to know the truth? Do you want to be engulfed by truth?
Lily	Oh, yes, I do. I definitely do.
Rita	Make room for God and he will reveal the truth to you personally. You don't need to travel through the labyrinths of creed, doctrine and dogma coming at you from every direction. If you want to find the way, I can tell you in three

words: Come to God—not to a plan, a system, or to an idea, nor to a man, but to the Spirit who reigns within your heart.

Jack

I agree with Rita, but let me add this: The modern churches have exalted the teaching and forgotten the Teacher. They have become consumed with preaching the creed and have forgotten the spirit that is the center of our faith and the very heart and core of our experience. Lots of people know about God. I used to know about him, but thank God, today I know him personally. You can know about him and still be lost, but if you call upon him to abide within, you will be saved from your lower-self.

Tony

I am going to confess to you that from my standpoint, the Bible is filled with the inexplicable. But I believe in God and take by faith the things that are incomprehensible to the mind. Then God proves that I am on the right path because of how I feel in my heart.

It is for us to make the effort.
The result is always in God's hands.

Mohandas K. Gandhi

After the intermission, less than half of the audience came back. Tony didn't mind, though. He sincerely believed that each person had the freedom to choose his or her own path. He respected their decision, but was glad some people chose to stay as he continued narrating the story.

Lily

I have a question, said Lily, glancing at Jack. How can you trust God? I have reached out to God many times before with requests, but I've never received any answers. As a matter of fact, it seems that the more I ask, the less I receive. The more I plead, the less I hear from him. To be quite honest with you, because of that silence from God, it is very hard for me to believe in him or trust him.

Rita

I understand. I used to feel the same way. I used to ask God for the things I wanted, but I never asked him if they were the things he wanted for me. I used to ask him to bless my plans, but never asked if these were the plans he had for me.

Jack

Rita is correct. Give God the chance to speak to you. God wants you to talk to him, but he also longs to talk to you. Usually, we ask God many questions, but we never listen quietly for him to answer. Instead, we get mad and blame him for his silence. We get discouraged because he doesn't answer when we want. Let me remind you, Lily, God's timing is not our timing.

Rita

I have learned that when we are aware of God, we can hear from God as well as God hears from us. He has many things to say to us, but we can't always bear them. We cannot comprehend or digest them until the Spirit teaches us. If we listen and allow him to teach us, the day will come when we understand.

Jack

Yes, when we allow the Spirit of God to be the center of our heart, he holds us at the center of his heart as well. When we have the realization that God abides within us, we are able to experience his essence in us, and we are also able to better understand his Spirit. What we see and comprehend on our own is so limited, but with the eyes and mind of the Spirit we comprehend differently; we commence to understand the things of God.

Lily

Tell me more, please?

Jack

When you become aware of the presence of God in your heart, Lily, you will understand. Those things that are incomprehensible from just reading and listening to lectures will be clear when you are filled with the Spirit. There is a big difference. It's one thing to be lectured to and another to be filled by the Spirit. The first one is knowledge and the second one is experience. The experience is something that starts to flow from things that God puts in your heart—things that you can't describe to others—things that belong only to you and him.

Tony

Lily closed her eyes.

Lily prayed

God, I am so confused. I hunger for your touch. I wish to know you. Open the eyes of my heart; I want to see you. Help me understand who you are. Help me to trust you. Help me to love you, not because of the things that you give me, but because of who you are—The Almighty!

Tony

When Lily opened her eyes, she felt good about her petitions to God. She had opened her heart to him and confessed her needs. She had asked from the bottom of her heart, to see God. She needed to see God! She longed to believe with conviction and trust him with all her heart. God had created her with this need for fulfillment that only God, and God alone, could fill.

'Good morning everybody,' said a lovely young woman. 'My name is Christy. May I join you?'

Of course, they all said.

Lily	Please sit down.
Christy	Thank you. I just wish to speak with you, said Christy, looking straight at Lily.
Lily	You do? Lily sort of nervously asked. How can I help you?
Christy	Well, it's just that you remind me of myself.
Lily	I remind you of you? Lily glanced at the rest of the group.
Christy	You remind me of myself when I was searching for God.
Lily thought	Gee, is my search that obvious?
Lily	How do I remind you?
Christy	I recognize the hunger of your heart and want to share something that I learned. May I?
Lily	Yes, of course. I'm willing to listen and learn.
Christy	I have learned that our hearts were made by God for his dwelling place. You will never be truly satisfied until He comes and dwells within!
Tony	Lily looked at Jack, who was shaking his head affirmatively.

I can understand what Christy is saying. In my experience, none but God could ever satisfy my soul. I was on a never-ending quest until I found God. Then, after I found him, my soul hungered for more and more of him. God made our hearts as a dwelling place for him, but I must be honest with you, I have allowed—and still do allow—fleshly impulses and desires to try to fill the hunger. But they only increase the void in my heart and the feeling of emptiness in my soul. Self-indulgence sometimes brought me pleasure, sometimes tears. But let me tell you, the burden of my tears was too heavy to bear. When I realized I was allowing self-indulgence to rob me of my soulfulness, I decided to wait for God to fill my cup. When I asked God to make my heart his dwelling place, I began to realize that only then would be I truly satisfied, and only then would the hunger of my heart for authenticity be completely met.

Jack	What else have you discovered in your journey? Jack asked Christy.

Christy	I have discovered that having faith is not how the world describes it.
Paul	What do you mean by that?
Christy	We live in a fleshly world directly in conflict with the spiritual or heavenly world. Faith does not come from the flesh or our human reasoning. Faith isn't the same as confidence. Instead, it is an energizing, creative power originating in and imparted by God's inner-presence.
Paul	I'm sorry, I don't quite understand what you mean by 'imparted by God?'
Christy	What I mean is that God is the faith! When God lives in our hearts, we have the faith that comes from God.
Lily	I still don't understand, admitted Lily.
Tony	Jack stepped in to help.
Jack	Faith in God is imparted by his indwelling—by the power of God who lives in us.
Lily	Hmm, that sort of makes sense. I remember all those times when I tried so hard to have faith, but nothing happened. I struggled so much with this issue. All my life I have been preached at that I have to have faith. If I don't, God will not be happy with me. That teaching has caused a lot of fear. Am I supposed to conjure up faith? Since I didn't have it, I believed I fell short of God's love and blessings. But now, after listening to you, I am beginning to understand why I haven't had faith. I haven't allowed God, who is the faith, to dwell in me. Am I on the right track? She looked around at them seeking confirmation.
Jack	Yes, that is exactly what I was saying! Jack nodded with eager approval.
Lily	Wow! Now tell me what else have you learned, Christy.
Christy	I have also learned that we don't find God's blessings by striving or struggling to attain them. We find them when we yield to God—when we surrender. Yielding yourself to God and trusting Him brings rest to your soul.
Jack	Amen to that! Only by yielding, not by striving, will you find his blessings. You need only to surrender.
Lily	But, how can anyone really surrender?
Rita	You can't, unless of course, you are conscious of God's indwelling presence.

Jack	That's correct. He alone can satisfy you. His light within you can guide you home. God's love can never be found by struggling, only by surrendering and by receiving it as a free gift directly from the heart of God to your own heart, which is one with his.
Lily	But when does that happen?
Jack	It happens when you have a personal relationship with God: when you learn to trust him, to love him, to listen to him; and most importantly, when you accept that God is love and that He has your best interest at heart.
Christy	I have discovered, that we learn as we go along. Scriptures say that we 'perish for lack of knowledge.' At first, I did not quite understand what that meant. But now, I do. God is the knowledge and wisdom, without him—without the awareness of God in us—we perish!
Lily	We perish?
Christy	Yes, we perish without the awareness of him, because without the knowledge of who he is in us and without his love instead of promises, we live in darkness and fear. We remain in bondage. God wants his people free, but freedom only comes when we allow God to be at the center of our hearts. We must know instead of believe, beyond a shadow of a doubt, that he is the provider of whatever we need to heal our souls.
Jack	Let me share something else. The most beautiful experience this side of the kingdom of God is to be led by the Spirit. Wisdom has emphasized to us, not once, but over and over again, that without divine direction, our efforts to have peace of mind and heart will be futile. Yet, the last thing we are willing to do is to give up our power to reason, which, according to us, is the principal tool used for our accomplishments. Next to that comes our will.
Lily	But Jack, God doesn't expect us to give up our ability to reason and our will, does he?
Lily thought	Please don't tell me he does because I won't be able to give them up. We are talking about my freedom to choose, for crying out loud!
Jack	No, Lily, God doesn't want to take away our freedom to choose, but he certainly wants us to switch from choices that are controlled by our own plans. He wants our choices to be what he would have guided us to do and our wants to be his wants, but we can only allow his control of our lives when we

have the consciousness that he loves us and has our best interest at heart. I wish that you could grasp what a difference that makes! If people were ready and willing to live their lives directed by the Spirit of God, they could escape so much harm and they'd realize that many of their terrible circumstances don't ever need to be. If we would ask God for guidance and direction as often as we ask for assistance, we wouldn't need to ask for help because our lives would already be in total union with him and we would be filled with his wisdom.

Tony

Let me share with you something personal. Once upon a time, I asked God to impart his presence and come into my life, but not to rule it. No! Oh, no, no, no! I didn't want to make him the master of my life. Instead, I considered him a sort of helper. When sorrow came, I ran to his side for comfort. If I misbehaved, I ran to him for forgiveness. If there was something that I wanted to do, I knelt down and devoutly asked for his help. When I was in the darkness, I cried for light. When I was in the storm, I asked for calm. When I was in the midst of trouble, I beseeched his peace. Clearly, I was living according to my own will and the attractive plans I had for my own life. But today, I know that God has my best interest at heart and that I don't even know what's best for me. I can honestly tell you that as a helper, God is good. As Lord and Master, he is better, but as the King reigning within, he is the best.

'Ladies and gentlemen,' the train conductor announced, 'we are approaching the City of The Spirit. We will be there shortly. I received a call from God. He indicated that there is someone on this train that has come especially to meet him. He says to tell you that he will be waiting at the door just for you.'

Lily's heart began to pound harder. Could God's message actually be for her? Was he going to be at the door to receive her? The thought sent a nervous shiver of excitement through her. She could hardly wait to meet God and get to know him on a personal level.

The train came to a full stop. People stood up, eager to enter the city. Everyone greeted Lily when they passed by her. Lily observed these people, thinking they were actually truly nice. They seemed loving and caring.

Lily stood up, excited to enter the City of the Spirit. She turned around, looking for Jack. He was standing behind her, smiling but with a tear in his eye. His look was one of gratitude that Lily had made it to this particular destination. Jack took her hand in his and brushed his thumb back and forth across her hand.

Jack	Lily, I cannot go there with you.
Lily	Why can't you, Jack?
Jack	Because this place belongs only to God and you.
Lily	Where will you be, Jack?
Jack	I will be going back to Religion City to help other people find their way here. Go on, Lily. God is waiting for you. Don't be afraid. God will not leave you nor forsake you. This is because God and you are One. Wherever you are, God is, because he dwells in you. Because he is your Higher Self, he cannot leave you. But you leave your own Higher Self when you choose to live your life without guidance from your own Spirit and choose the ego or mortal mind to be in charge. He is loving, kind, patient, and understanding, and since you are created in his image and likeness, so are you. You will find shelter, refuge, peace, and rest in this city. You have arrived, Lily. You have arrived at the fountain. You will no longer thirst.
Lily	But Jack, I don't want you to go, she pleaded.
Jack	I am not leaving you for good, Lily. I will be waiting for you to share with me your experience with God, but you must go alone to the City of the Spirit.
Tony	Lily's eyes were brimming with tears.
Lily	Thank you, Jack. Thank you for showing me the way. Thank you for your patience and your love. You were the answer to my prayers. Lily embraced him tenderly. Jack looked at her with those blue eyes that reflected a soul in total union with God.
Jack	I love you, Lily!
Lily	I love you too, Jack!

We all wander through life united by the bond of creation and become
brothers through gratitude. We have much to be thankful for.
Let each of us talk to the same Supreme Being in his own way.

Chief Dan George

Tony	When Lily stepped off the train, she was overwhelmed by the presence of God's Spirit. She felt carefree and vibrant. She felt God's love alive in her heart. This was new—and a bit awkward for her. She was not used to being loved in such a way, but at the same time, it felt so wonderful and incredibly refreshing! Here was a place of so much delight, something Lily never experienced before. Her longing—her unfulfilled longing—seemed to have come to an end.
	The City of the Spirit was magnificent. Each visitor had a special place in the heart of God. Peace, Love, Joy, Forgiveness, Trust, Mercy, Responsibility, Humility, Conscience, Self-control, Hope, Patience and Understanding were all there. They were welcoming everyone into God's dwelling place, without prejudice.
	Welcome home, they cheered in unison, causing Lily to smile. Suddenly, right in front of her eyes, they all blended together like a tornado funnel cloud, united as one. At first, Lily didn't understand what was happening, but it all became clear, as at that precise moment Christ appeared.
Christ	Dear ones, all of you who desire a deeper walk with God, come and enter into his presence through me. I am the way, and I am so pleased to have you here! It is God's desire to manifest himself to you, to impart abundant grace, and to help you see, so that you may give yourself permission to accept and enjoy his presence. You all are very dear to God.
Tony	Lily wasn't so sure about that.
Lily thought	If I am so dear to God, how come he abandoned me?
Christ	God never abandoned you, Lily. Never! You just thought he did because he didn't answer the way you wanted.
Lily	Yeah, but I needed to hear from him. I cried out to him, over and over again, and he didn't comfort me. I prayed to him from the depths of my soul, and he ignored me.
Tony	Lily wavered between being hurt and being broken.
Christ	He did not ignore you, Lily. He heard your cry. That's why you are here today, as an answer to your prayers.
Tony	As we have already heard, God's time is not our time.

Christ	You prayed for wisdom and understanding. You prayed for love and peace. You prayed for a place where you could rest from the pressures of the world. You prayed for water to quench the thirst of your soul. Lily, you will find all that in me. Allow me to lead you into communion with God. God is the Source of all things, but I am the one who will open the door for you. I can give you water—living water—water so completely satisfying that once you drink it, you will never, ever thirst again.
Tony	I can testify to that. Before I entered into a personal relationship with Christ, I was anxious. I was worried. But when I had my first glimpse of the light within me, when I savored the essence of God, even if it was for an instant, I discovered the nectar of life. It was so sweet and tasty that my soul desired more. The living water—the nectar—was available to me with no limits. I drank of it. I drink of it now, more often than before, and when I forget to accept the living water offered by Christ, I remind myself that love lives in me and the feeling of anxiety and worrying subside and I experience that the thirst goes away.
Christ	Would you like to take my hand and walk with me, Lily?
Tony	Lily looked at him. She was amazed to realize how wonderful she felt in his presence.
Lily	Yes, I do want to take your hand and follow you.
Tony	Christ and Lily walked hand in hand towards the center of the city. Lily kept looking at him, and he kept smiling at her with so much love in his eyes. What wonderful moments these were! Lily was speechless. She could not get over how alive and new Christ made her feel. In his presence, she felt the most unusual desire to be the best that she could be. She realized that holding grudges against other people was just not worth it. Anger lost its stronghold in Lily's heart. She found herself able to open her heart's door to forgiveness and trust. As a result, a big load was lifted from her shoulders.
Lily	Wow! What a place this is! Lily looked around in amazement. Oh, Christ, she said, looking at him with gratitude in her eyes, thank you for coming to welcome me at the door. Thank you for inviting me to walk with you, for guiding me into the knowledge and understanding of God—the knowledge and understanding of my own Self.
Christ	Christ smiled. I am very happy you finally got here. I want you to know that I am not complete without you.

Lily	How can it be that you are not complete without me? You are God's Son. You have everything. You don't need me-e-e!
Christ	Oh, but I do. I do need you, Lily. I need you to be in perfect union with me. You are a part of who I am. That is why without you, I am not complete. Yes, I am God's son, and so are you. According to you, I have everything. But I don't. I have almost everything.
Lily	For crying out loud, how could you say you have 'almost everything?'
Christ	I don't have you, Lily. You are not yet aware of who I am. You have just heard about me, but you don't know me, and without you, I am not complete because you and I are one. Do you understand, Lily?
Lily	No, I guess not.
Tony	Lily was uncomfortable and embarrassed. Christ chuckled.
Christ	Are you feeling embarrassed, Lily? Don't be. As I said, you don't know me.
Lily	I know, but I want to know you, Lily excitedly began to explain. I want to feel the Spirit of God in my heart. I don't want just to talk about God. I want to experience him. I don't want to be afraid of God. I want to be in awe and respect of him instead. I have walked a long road to find God, and now that I can accept that you are the one who opens the door to the heart of God, now that I know that you, the Christ within me, are the fountain for which I thirst, I intend to get to know you. I plan to drink of your living waters until I am totally satisfied.
Christ	Does that mean that you are inviting me to come into your heart? Christ asked her, with a radiant and expectant smile.
Lily	Oh, yes, I am inviting you in. I am asking you to take my hand and guide me, because I am blind. I am requesting that you hold me in your loving arms, because I am afraid. I ask you to show me your power, so that I may believe. I am pleading that I may allow myself to accept and believe that you love me, in the unconditional way only you can love. Is that possible, Christ?
Christ	It's not only possible, but it is already done. I will never let go of your hand. I promise. But, make sure that you don't let go of mine, and if you do, don't condemn yourself, Lily, this is a process, just come back as many times as it is necessary. God never judges you. It is you who judges yourself. God's Spirit lives in you and will guide you, if you let it. My arms are wide

open for you whenever you need them. You can find shelter and refuge in me. You don't need to be afraid anymore. I am with you—in you—forever. If you walk with me and learn to wait upon me, you will be able to experience God's power. The more you see, the more you will believe. The more you believe, the more you will see. I love you, Lily. I love you with an unconditional love. Please understand that I don't love you because you are *good*. If I were to love you because you are good, it wouldn't be unconditional love, now would it? I love you simply because you are Lily. God and I delight in you.

Lily

But, ah... Christ. I am so imperfect. I make a multitude of mistakes. I am often unloving and selfish, even self-centered. I am a human being with too many shortcomings. I'm certainly not worthy of this special treatment.

Christ

You may not think you are worth very much, but let me assure you, God thinks you are. You feel unworthy of God, Lily, because you are trying too hard to compare yourself to him. You must stop doing that. Let go of that habit. You will never be able to measure up to God. He is the Almighty! He is greater than you can even imagine. Rest assured, my dear Lily, that God does not weigh you with human scales, he does not compute your worth according to human standards. If you keep trying to measure up to him, I am afraid you won't be able to be one with God, because you'll always believe that you are not deserving of him. There are so many souls who have wandered away. Even you have strayed because you didn't believe God loves you or accepts you, because of your faults. It's impossible to be perfect; you need not be. God's thoughts are not your thoughts. Let God be God, Lily.

Lily

So, what am I supposed to do to change?

Christ

Come to me with your broken heart and open mind. You have stayed away because of your confusion regarding who I am. You have kept a distance between us because of your misconceptions and imperfections. You no longer have to do that, Lily. I will reveal my unconditional love for you. I will also cleanse and restore your heart, and you will pardon yourself for every wrongdoing. I have nothing to forgive you for. My dear Lily, he continued with a sweet, sweet smile, there isn't a broken heart that I cannot heal. Perplexities and confusion can be made clear. Miserable lives can be made joyful. There's not a problem I cannot solve. Nothing, Lily, nothing is impossible for me.

Lily, I know you are imperfect, everyone is. I know your
heart needs to be made new. Every heart does, not just yours.
No one is completely good; no, not one—only our Creator is.
The change of heart takes place while you are walking on
your spiritual journey. Each day you walk a little further
along the path. With each step you take, you grow wiser,
more compassionate, more loving, and more trusting. You
become aware of my presence all around you, and as a result,
you become increasingly sensitive to hearing my voice. Be
patient and gentle with yourself, Lily. Allow my way to
unfold before you. My way is best for you. I love you more
than you can ever imagine. Let me guide you when the way is
unclear. Let me strengthen you when the way is difficult. On
your spiritual journey there are no mistakes, only lessons to
be learned.

Tony

It was such a relief for me to hear Christ talk about God.
Christ helped me understand what God is all about. God,
he said, is not a malicious and vengeful God, who is
holding a whip, ready to strike you if you make a
mistake. No, not at all! In God, I discovered an inner
presence that is loving, caring, and understanding; who
loves you with an unconditional love; who is available to
you at all times; whose spirit lives in you, and therefore,
you can find shelter and refuge in your own heart.

Christ and Lily sat next to each other. She was enjoying his
companionship. She was resting in his presence. She felt
peaceful and joyful, secure and protected. Lily felt at ease
asking Christ the questions for which her heart needed
answers. Who better than he to answer?

Lily

Christ, why is it that most of us just don't understand who
you are?

Christ

That is because you want to know the reason before you
start. I want you to start before I give you the reason. Lily,
you want to believe through understanding. I want you to
understand through believing. When you begin to see and
comprehend things you normally cannot comprehend, it is
the Spirit who is revealing it to you. The beauty of my
existence in your heart is its power to overcome all
circumstances in your life—to be saved from the hell in
which you live. Hell is separation from me. Without me, you
are alone and have no place to find refuge. Without me, you
are lonely and afraid, walking aimlessly without direction.
But with me, what a different story. I can turn your darkness
into light. I can fill your empty heart with joy and peace. I
can take your hand and lead you to where you can find the

abundance stored for all those who trust in me. Walk with me and I will grant you spiritual gifts. I will give your mind an understanding of every good path and your heart an abundance of love, joy, and wisdom.

Tony

As my own spiritual awareness grew, I became better at recognizing the message from God. He has promised that when we seek wisdom, we will receive it, but we must ask in faith and have no doubts; for he who has doubts is a man of two minds, undecided in every step he takes, like the waves of the sea, driven by the wind and tossed around. I believe God wants us to grow in understanding. God wants us to know the truth directly from him. He wants to give us his wisdom so we may understand who he is, and stop the doubts.

Christ

Lily, even though you feel unworthy, in the eyes of God, you are perfect for the day.

Lily

How can that be? What do you mean by 'perfect for the day'?

Christ

You are perfect for the day, Lily, because God is the sculptor of your heart. When you give your heart to God, God begins to mold it one small piece at a time. Remember this: if you abide in God, you will see that every day you are in the place where you are supposed to be for the evolution of your soul. Tomorrow is another day. With every passing day, you'll become better and better—not in behavior, but in understanding, and as a result the behavior automatically changes. Just be still and know that God loves you, and he has your best interest at heart.

Lily thought

Now that just seems too good to be true.

Christ

Who told you it has to be difficult?

Tony

Keith once said to me:

Keith

Tony, it's extremely hard if you follow God based on man's rules, standards and interpretations of who he is. Religious people will put too much pressure on you. But, it is easier when you get closer to God and allow him, by your own will, to guide you. He will speak directly to your heart. He might choose to talk to you through someone else, but the thing to keep in mind is that when God speaks to you, *you'll know* that he has spoken. God can speak to you the same way he speaks to others. Are you any different than someone else that God speaks to? Are you? No, you are not.

Christ	My dear Lily, rest your head upon my heart, and let me hold you in my arms. I know what you need and I will provide for you and lift every burden. Do not be afraid to put your life into my care and if you are trusting and depend on me for guidance and direction, I will give it. I will walk in front of you and clear the way. Yield your whole being to me, Lily. I will shelter you and protect you. I will be the rock of your life and your strong support.
Tony	Lily was looking at Christ in awe. Christ's eyes revealed so much love for her. She got close to him and sat in his lap, placing her head upon his chest. Christ's hand was softly and tenderly caressing her curls.
Christ	Lily, he whispered, you are precious and dear to my heart. *Everyone is.* I love you more than you can ever comprehend. I have waited so long to gather you in my arms and hold you close to my Spirit. Now you are in my embrace, rest here. You will experience God's presence in your heart, and you shall rejoice in all kind of situations, because God will share with you his love, his peace, and his joy regardless of your circumstances—regardless of your behavior. God only looks at your heart, and he knows that your heart is pure because he created it. God sees no flaw in you, Lily, but you believe, as everyone else does, that you have so many flaws, and therefore, you are not worthy of God, and as a result of that belief, you cannot experience God's presence, because God is love and before you can experience love, you must learn to love yourself with all your flaws and stop treating yourself so unkindly.
Lily	What have I done to deserve such a gift?
Christ	Nothing. It is a gift. It is available for everyone who is ready to accept it. You are ready. You have sought God with all your heart, and you have found him in me, Lily. God gives his love, his peace, and his joy to everyone. But only those who long for a closer relationship with him can experience it. I pour out wisdom and understanding to those who pour out their lives—their minds—to me. But you must know, that in the fullness of time, everyone will find their way back to the City of the Spirit.
Tony	Lily was weeping. It felt so wonderful to be in the arms of Christ. She surrendered and let go of her fear and opened her heart to receive his love, his kindness, and his teachings.
Christ	Your heart shall be filled. You shall be pleased. Do not be overly concerned with the things of the world, for they are temporary. Do not be worried as to what you will eat or wear,

for God knows what you need, and you can rest assured that he will supply them if you let him. Look at me, Lily, lift your eyes to mine and allow God's will to take place in your life. Pay attention to my guidance and direction, be attentive and keep your ears and your heart open to hear my voice whispering in the depths of your being. Listen to me; my Spirit will bring you revelation and understanding, light and wisdom, and as a result, your hunger and thirst after righteousness shall be satisfied.

Our fear and emptiness are not part of his plan. Old hurts and old wounds created them. If you could see yourself through God's eyes, you would see that you are completely loved and completely protected.

Deepak Chopra

Tony

Lily went back to her cabin with so much more knowledge and understanding than the day she began her journey. She had discovered so much, she could hardly wait to tell Jack all about it. There was a knock at the front door. It was Jack.

Lily

Jack, it's so nice to see you! Please come in. Lily hugged him tenderly. Oh, Jack, I am so glad you are here. I wish to share everything I've learned. She was excited about sharing because Jack was a good listener. He understood and related to her.

Tony

Jack looked at her, winked, and playfully commanded, You'd better! I want to hear everything. Jack made himself comfortable on the sofa. Lily offered him a cup of coffee and a piece of her favorite strawberry cheesecake.

Lily

The more time I spend in the presence of Christ, the more I learn about him and about myself. The more I learn about him, the closer I get to him. I am experiencing a transformation, a change of heart. Jack, I find myself trusting in God. I am experiencing the willingness to learn more about him. I believe God has prepared me. He has enabled me to open the door of my heart to the Holy Spirit, and now I am willing to follow his lead. Although thoughts of fear and unbelief try to hinder me or make me stumble, my determination to know God's gentle presence within is far greater.

Jack

I totally understand, Lily. I walk with God, and as I walk with him, I discover and experience more and more of the love of God—the peace of God. My trust and belief in God take all my burdens away.

Lily   Do you know what's so amazing to me, Jack? Realizing just how easy it is to forgive others as well as myself for all the mistakes I have made, and no doubt will make, in my life. What a relief it is not to condemn myself for failing to live up to expectations of others and my own. It tastes so sweet not to be overly concerned about how I am reflected in the mirror of people's minds, and by that I mean, it does not matter whether people agree with me or not.

Jack   That's true, Lily. As you walk with Christ and allow the Spirit of God—which is Christ himself—to live in your heart and guide your every step, you will find yourself lighter and freer. Things that were so important to you before lose their significance, and afterwards you realize what a weight you were carrying. In my experience, I found it almost unbelievable at first that my belief in Christ could make me feel the way I feel—free! Free of my fears and insecurities; free to reach out to him; free to ask him any questions; free to be honest and pour my heart totally and completely out to him about my doubts and concerns. After walking closely to Christ for a while, I found out for myself that Christ is indeed who he says he is! He is the one who opens the door to the heart of God in me. When I realized this, then I was able to let go and allow God to take care of my life. I learned to trust God with all my heart and to love him with all my soul.

Tony   Lily was surprised to realize that she could relate to Jack.

Lily   Unbelievable! It is just so unbelievable. If someone would have told me that one day, I would find myself in the place where I am today, I would have said, 'You're out of your mind. God doesn't care. Christ is for freaks.' Yes. That's exactly what I would have said. But I've been wrong. To understand what Christ is all about is a marvelous thing.

You know what else, Jack? I finally understand there is nothing, absolutely nothing, I can do to earn the love of God. God's love is a gift and I am telling you, I am willing to open it and enjoy it. Isn't that something?

Jack   That is wonderful, Lily. I rejoice for you. Jack was jubilant. Do you want me to tell you what made my life a lot easier? Understanding that God's plans for my life are far better than the plans I have for myself. When I was enlightened with this pearl of wisdom, I was able to allow God to direct my path, to make him the captain of my ship and master of my life—master of my mind—and with that, I found the rest I had been searching for.

Tony

What makes my life easier, is the understanding that I could never be good, let alone perfect. I know I will make mistakes and fall short before my concept of God. I also know that no matter how far I fall, I will never be out of God's reach. I know the Spirit of God will always be there to hold me, teach me, console me, and help me to forgive myself. It doesn't matter any longer what other people think of me. All that matters is that God loves me just the way I am, and I am learning to love myself as God loves me. As I continue on my walk with God, he will teach me and equip me with wisdom and understanding, so that I may be better, so that I may act better and think better, but perfect? Never.

Lily

What a relief it is, Jack, to know that I don't have to be good to be loved by God. How mistaken I have been—comparing God's love with the love of man. Men's love is based on performance. The better I am, the more they love me. What a pressure! But it is not so with God. God's love is unconditional, and that kind of love makes me want to be the best I can be.

Tony

Lily let out a deep sigh.

Lily

I know walking with God doesn't guarantee everything will be okay. It doesn't even guarantee I will be free of problems and heartache. No, I'm sure it doesn't. We all have pleasant experiences but painful ones as well. Pleasant experiences make life delightful. Painful experiences lead to growth. What is guaranteed, though, is that there will always be a place where I can find shelter until the storm passes by. It's assured that my soul can be at peace, even in the midst of adversity. I have a new belief that although I might become sad, I won't be miserable.

Tony

Now I understand God's peace. I remember those days when I looked forward to a vacation away from the rat race and find a couple of weeks of real peace away from the pressures of every day. But now I know that peace is a spiritual quality of the heart and mind. It is not the absence of responsibility and hard work. Peace is a state of mind that we possess in the midst of all the chaos and conflict of every day because of our belief in God. I realized that I have a choice. It's up to me to choose God's peace and serenity when the heavy clouds of life come down on me. If I do—if I choose God's peace—God's peace will abide in me and my soul will be sheltered from the heavy winds, and I will be resting in the hand of God while the storm rages and howls.

Jack	That is what I call the peace of God. God radiates his peace while he dwells within us. It is his presence that inspires it. It is the consciousness that he is there—in our hearts—that gives us the calm within. God had been trying to get your attention for such a long time, but you were not ready to see.
Lily	I know, and I can't blame myself for it, because now I am aware that everything happens according to the plan of my soul for its own evolution. In other words, everything happens in the fullness of time.
Tony	There is a calling to which we are often unaware. God invites man to a life of close union and communion with him. Spiritual maturity doesn't happen overnight. Godly understanding doesn't come all at once. Knowledge and spiritual aptitude are not given in the twinkling of an eye. It takes time and growth to get there.
Lily	Oh, Jack, it has been an extraordinarily long journey.
Jack	And it continues, Lily, because you are here to learn how to get rid of the impurities of the human mind, not of the heart, because the heart cannot be impure. Sometimes that takes a while too.
Lily	Jack, am I talking your ear off?
Jack	No, Lily, you aren't, he said smiling kindly. You can talk to me as long as you want. That's what I am here for—to listen to you.
Tony	Lily continued, and she spoke with conviction.
Lily	I believe we all have the right to reach out to God in our own personal way. Do you believe that, Jack?
Jack	I sure do. That is exactly what I did. I reached out in a personal way, and I found him. Yes, I did. I found him, right in the center of my heart. That is where God dwells, in the center, in the core, in the depths of our being.
Lily	You know what else? Since the day I understood who God is, especially the fact that God doesn't punish or judge, my life has changed tremendously. I grew so much in my spiritual search, and I discovered the love that I always longed for. That love is within me! I thought a special person was the source of my love, joy, and happiness. I was wrong. God is the source of love because God is love. When I found God's love in my heart, I also found joy, peace, happiness and serenity.

Tony

You may be thinking that's too good to be true. I understand because I thought so myself for a long time. But nevertheless, it is true. To be in union with God and to enjoy God's love dwelling in me brings peace and deliverance wherever I may go. The greatest gem of wisdom I have come to know is that God doesn't care about what I do for him, but what I allow him to do for me and through me. When I allow God to do for me, I am allowing his plan—his will—to take place in and through my life and there is liberty in that.

Lily

My newly acquired understanding of God is helping me to set myself free. All my wants, needs, desires, and concerns are losing their strength. Issues that used to be so important to me such as 'I am right and you are wrong; it's my way or the highway; I don't need anyone; I can do everything alone,' took a lot of energy out of me. There are things that are more vital to me now, such as living a life filled with love and understanding for myself and for others. I have learned to choose my battles. Some are worth fighting; some are not. It is no longer important to me to be right. It is more important to have peace of mind and heart. I know now, after a lot of weariness, disillusionment, and heartache, that life and people, especially people, are not always the way I would like them to be. If I expect them to be who and what I want them to be, I will be fighting a losing battle. Instead, I simply cease pushing for people to change. Giving up is the best way to accept people as they are.

Jack

I also found freedom knowing that life is not intended to be the same for everyone. Before this truth was revealed to me, I felt bad for people's circumstances, even my own. I questioned God's existence because of the hard lives I saw around me. 'If there is a God,' I questioned, 'why does he allow this to happen?' Now I know we all have our challenges. Some of us have it harder than others. I don't understand exactly why, but I am no longer stuck trying to understand some of the mysteries of life. Instead, I press forward by applying the things that I do understand, which is that we all have access to God's strength, and each is responsible for accepting God's power in order to improve our spiritual lives. God is available for everyone as a refuge and as a shelter during the storms that crash against our shores. No one is exempt from the heavy winds, and no one is exempt from his loving embrace.

Lily

I struggled with that too. I guess maybe everyone does. It is very hard to see God in the midst of adversity. We live our lives in parts, but God sees the whole picture. It's not until every piece or part falls into place that we understand and see that God was always there, in command of everything. But as I realized along the way, that is a hard pill to swallow until all the pieces fit together. What used to be uncomfortable is now very comfortable. I enjoy being alone, Lily confided. I find myself yearning for solitude. There is something so utterly fantastic and spiritual about solitude. It gives me the opportunity to reflect on my life, my friends, my work, or simply to be still so I may listen to the sound of silence or to the sweet voice within that whispers, 'I love you, Lily. I will never leave you nor forsake you. I am with you, forever. Let my love and peace run through you like a torrent, washing away all the poison of your heart and soul. Let my wisdom flow through you like a river. Allow me to renew your thoughts and beliefs and cleanse away all your poisonous memories.' The sweet and loving voice of God's Spirit within me is like a warm comforter on a cold night, and it makes all the difference in my world.

Jack

The way I see it, the purpose of life is to find God in our lives and in our hearts. Then we will be transformed into his image. When we have the awareness that the spirit of God is in our heart and soul, we automatically have God's wisdom. God's wisdom is not something to be attained, but is something that is imparted. It is given, not earned. We must keep in mind that the wisdom of God is not the same as the wisdom of the world. Human wisdom often turns out to be silliness in the sight of God. To know God's wisdom, we have to be freed from the wisdom of the world. The wisdom God grants is not the product of human thinking; it is rather the small, sweet voice of God speaking directly in our soul; it is the revelation of God's Spirit to us. This type of wisdom surpasses all human knowledge and understanding.

Such wisdom is not the result of study; it is rather a matter of reaching the point where we are ready to let go of the baggage we carry in our mind and allow our Spirit to emerge. To find God's wisdom is a process that takes place within; it is something that happens internally and not externally, as most of us have been programmed to believe that the peace of God can come through exterior forces. It can't. The wisdom of God is the reflection of the mind of God. Once we find it, then we are to enjoy each day and live a life filled with love, peace, and serenity.

Lily

Oh, Jack, I love what you just said.

Tony

A meek smile spread on Jack's face.

Jack

Let me leave you with something else to ponder. God's will is not constrained within the rules of any formal religion. There is no end to God's wisdom. God deals with us as individuals. In every individual heart there is a need for the wisdom of God, and in every life there is the possibility of knowing the wisdom that comes from him. Always remember that wisdom comes from above, but the revelation comes from within. Faith in Christ brings wisdom and love into your heart. Life is particularly short and sooner or later will come to an end. Lily, when my time comes, I want to leave this world with the certainty that I learned what I came to learn: to discover the love that I am. I came to learn self-realization. It is only when I allow the love that I am to emerge, I may be in the position to love my neighbor as myself.

I feel good because the world is right. Wrong!
The world is right because I feel good.

Anthony deMello

Tony

Jack left and Lily lingered by the window, taking in the beautiful day that God made. In her heart was the conviction that God dwelt within. After a long journey, she understood the meaning of God—the meaning of love. As a result, she established a close and intimate relationship with him, a relationship that belonged only to the two of them. Lily knew her heart was right in the sight of God. No matter how she behaved in the eyes of the world, in the eyes of God—in her own eyes—she was just where she needed to be at that moment in time. She was so grateful for the awareness of walking with him, and honored to see him through the eyes of the Spirit. Lily discovered Christ to be a friend, one who listened to her when she needed someone to listen. Lily had come to the realization that she'd been trying to find in people what only God could give her. She found refuge in Christ. She found rest in Christ. She found freedom in Christ. She found forgiveness in Christ. She found love, peace and understanding in Christ, and the gray blanket of grief that had been wrapped around her soul for so long was in the process of being dismantled.

Lily walked toward her rocking chair and sat in the glow of the fireplace; her heart peaceful. She found what she was searching for—the connection with the fountain! The Spirit was sitting on the throne of her heart, and there was union with God.

Outside the door were those unpleasant beings: Anger, Frustration, Despair, Insecurity, Fear, Temptation, Indulgence, Gluttony, and Guilt, among others. There they were, looking through the window, knocking at the door, wanting to come in. They wouldn't go away! They would always be there, ready to seize the first opportunity to get back into Lily's heart. But Lily was no longer alone. Now she had God—she had Love—who gave her the strength to keep the door closed, if she chose. And if she chose not to, she could count on the unconditional love of God. Lily learned that the spiritual path is about progress, not perfection.

Lily was aware that these feelings had no power over her unless she gave in to them, and believe you me, she will at times. Oh, yes, she will. But the difference was that now she had God to console her and heal her wounds. She had a place to go. She could run to the loving arms of God, which are always open to embrace her and hold her close to his loving heart, regardless.

Lily could hear Christ's inaudible voice saying, 'Talk to me. I am your best friend, no one, absolutely no one will love you the way I do, and no one will ever snatch you out of my hand. Your heart is pure, and the pure of heart shall see God.'

Lily's smile lit up the room. She closed her eyes and rested. She had found the fountain, and out of her innermost being were flowing rivers of living water.

Tony

Ladies and gentlemen, I'm going to ask you to ponder the following: Is Lily going to stay there in the Promised Land? Is she going to be able to turn to the fountain within to guide her and sustain her? Or is her intellectual mind—her lower-self, the ego mind, the mind where fear abides—going to push and pull her around like before?

For me? I went back and forth from one to the other and to be totally honest, I still do. As we have already heard, the mystery of self-realization is a process, not a race. Life is a journey of discovery—of self-discovery—and in order to remain afloat in the living waters, we must constantly turn and *face* the obstacles *we* have placed in our path. We have placed them there with our thoughts and beliefs, with our needs and desires, and with our fear and guilt. We must be willing to observe ourselves without judgment, guilt, punishment or condemnation, because only when we observe ourselves with God's Love we are able to recognize these obstacles and be rescued from our worse enemy—our lower self.

Epilogue

The lights came up and the heavy curtains, the color of red wine, closed behind Tony as he stepped forward. For a while, applause filled the auditorium, and as it died down, Tony spoke.

Tony   Ladies and gentlemen, thank you for your attention. It was a pleasure narrating the story of Lily for you.

One of the spectators raised his hand.

Tony   Do you have a question, sir? And what is your name?

David   Yes, I do. I'm David. I enjoyed you telling the story of Lily because you seem to understand and relate to her. You display what I would imagine freedom to be like. So how did you come to the heart of God?

Tony   After having the experience of meeting Christ personally, and by that, I mean, understanding who he is in me, and realizing the truth of his teaching about the kingdom of God, I knocked at the door of heaven—in me—and reached out to God with a humble heart. I came to God like a child and poured my whole heart to him, and in time, he answered. And he still does; it's an everyday thing.

David   So you personally believe that Christ is the only way to the heart of God?

Tony   Let me put it this way for you, David. Life is a mystery, and no one can tell you the truth, you have to discover it for yourself. In my pursuit of God, I tried many different avenues, different approaches, and always—without fail—I returned to the same place: to a life filled with frustration, fear, guilt, and uncertainty. I was able to find only temporary relief for the pain my soul felt, and had little courage to face tomorrow. I tried so hard to find my way to the heart of God, applying every technique I was taught in order to find peace in my soul. I couldn't make it work. I could not make the connection until I understood the nature of Christ.

David   And what is the nature of Christ?

Tony   The nature of Christ is the essence of God. Take a close look at the man called Jesus, and you will see in him the reflection of the Spirit of God. Jesus had the Spirit of God within, and that's why he was able to love unconditionally. Jesus was kind and non-judgmental. He knew how to forgive because the Spirit of God is forgiveness. Because Jesus knew the Father, he could trust, follow, and rest in the midst of the heavy storms. Jesus possessed love, peace, joy, and a strength that could not be broken; he displayed the nature of God. He knew where he came from and to whom he belonged. That's why he asked that we follow him because he knew the way—the way to the realization that the kingdom of God dwells within.

But I found that I could not bond with God until I realized, through the message of Jesus, interpreted for me by the Spirit of God—in me—that God loves every one of us just the way we are. Every philosophy I read about God spoke to me about him, but I didn't realize that I was truly loved unconditionally. I don't know about you, but I needed to know—to feel—that I am loved, and loved unconditionally, without judgment and criticism.

However, I did not come to that awareness and the realization that the kingdom of God is within me until Christ came into my heart. It was Christ who made me known to the Father and made the Father known to me. It was through Christ that I discovered the love of God for me, and for you. It is through Christ that I believe in love and peace. I believe in miracles and in rivers of hope. It is Christ who gives me faith in things I cannot see. His presence within me allows me to see what the power of God can do when it seems impossible for me to make it through the heavy storms that hit my shores. It is through Christ that I am able to lift my eyes to heaven and ask God to pour over me, and over you, his love, his care, and his blessings. Because of Christ, I can ask God to hold me together, to clear the way, and to turn on the light within me, to extinguish the darkness of my soul. The message that Christ brought into my heart—the promises of unconditional love—are like a breath of fresh air that clears away my anxiety, doubts, and fear. Based on that, I must say that for me the answer is yes. I came to the conclusion that only Christ himself could satisfy the desires of my heart, banish my doubts, and take away all my worries and fears. Christ is the only way I found to the heart of the Father, and having Christ in my heart and in my mind brings me more tranquility than I've found in any other spiritual pursuit. Having the awareness that Christ is in my heart gives me a feeling of truth and being whole. Now I know that Christ comes to bring us joy, love and peace.

Tony noticed that David was not very convinced. There were visible signs of skepticism—resistance. Tony paused for a second. He looked at David with love and care.

Tony   David, he said in a soft, tender voice, even though you don't yet appear to believe, I think you want to believe in something greater than yourself. Otherwise, you wouldn't have stayed until the end of this story. Believe me when I say that God is love and that love will fill the aching need in your heart. The Christ within will make it possible to live life in a new way. You can have peace and joy in your heart. You can be free from the guilt and pain of your past and the anxieties of tomorrow. The message of Christ leads to victory and peace. If you are hungering for love, peace, acceptance, and serenity in your heart and soul, you need Christ. When you open the door of your heart to Christ, you will experience that God has always been there, and you will allow God to shower you—through your experience—with the fruits of his Spirit, and you will realize that you are indeed an heir to his kingdom.

Tony's eyes welled with tears as he said to David, and everyone listening,

It is my experience that Christ can not only change a man's life, but he can change a man's heart. I hope you'll get to know him too! One of the most wonderful things I have discovered about the ministry of Jesus is the truth that Christ came to set us free. I was in such bondage to others as well as to those hindrances and heaviness I fabricated within myself. When Christ came into my life—when I was ready to receive him—the shackles that kept me in bondage were broken, and I experienced freedom for the first time in my life. All I can tell you is that I know I have found the truth for myself, because I have love, peace, joy, acceptance, and serenity in my mind, heart and soul. I know you will find it for yourself, too.

With these final words, Tony stepped behind the curtain and the show concluded. The Announcer thanked everyone for coming and the audience began to make its way out into the night.

David sat quietly for a while as the others filed out. The evening had left him with a feeling of longing. He walked out of the theater into the street. Suddenly, a familiar voice greeted him. "Can I walk you to the station?" said Tony, putting on his hat.

THE END

www.ingramcontent.com/pod-product-compliance
Lightning Source LLC
LaVergne TN
LVHW051558080426
835510LV00020B/3039